Blue-jean cafetière cosy, page 49

Creative Christmas Gifts

Creative Christmas Gifts

Perfect ideas for gifts to make at home

ANNETTE CLAXTON · MARY LAWRENCE · CHERYL OWEN

NH

NEW
HOLLAND

First published in the UK in 1991 by
New Holland (Publishers) Ltd, 37 Connaught Street, London W2 2AZ

ISBN 1 85368 127 X

Editors: Jo Finnis; Elizabeth Rowe
Contributors: Robert Claxton (knife block; book-ends); Linda Grey
(herbal coat hanger); Christina Newholm (miniature boxes)
Designer: Phil Gorton
Cover design: Phil Gorton; Paul Wood
Photographs: Steve Tanner
Illustrations: Kathy Gummer; Cheryl Owen; Andy Waterman; Geoff Denney
Phototypeset by Bookworm Typesetting, Manchester, England
Originated by Scantrans Pte Ltd
Printed and bound in Singapore by Kyodo Printing Co (Singapore) Pte Ltd

Contents

ACKNOWLEDGEMENTS
The publishers would like to thank Tim and Hilary Derouet for providing the location for photography at Thruxted Oast, Chartham, Canterbury, Kent; and Helen Sheane Wallcoverings, 35 Connaught Street, London, W2 for providing the fruity fabric pictured on pages 20–21.

CHAPTER 1
Decorative Gifts

We present a collection of unusual gifts that are permanent home decorations, though some are specially designed to be revamped or replenished at intervals throughout the year, for added variety and interest. Others can be displayed annually at Christmas time and make ideal gifts for those individuals who often pose problems when it comes to choosing something appropriate: business contacts, distant relatives or neighbours.

The tree traditionally forms the focal point of yuletide decorations in the home and we have selected some eye-catching and entertaining tree gifts – both fun to make and receive. They can serve as a foretaste of the more substantial family gifts. Alternatively, save them for a final treat when the festivities are drawing to a close.

Three kings from Persian lands afar

This regal trio, each member bearing a handsome gift, makes an impressive group to adorn a mantlepiece or table. Let your imagination run free when trimming their crowns and gifts; embellish them as simply or as flamboyantly as you wish. Because of the delicate trimmings, these kings are purely decorative and not for children to play with.

Requirements

Three small cardboard tubes approximately 11.5 cm (4¹/₂ in) in length and 5 cm (2 in) in diameter
Scraps of satin, sequinned and other exotic fabrics
Fabric glue
Three pipe-cleaners
A stapler
Pale pink card
Household glue
Scraps of brown and black fur fabric
Toy filling or polyester wadding
Gold card
Beads, gold cord, giftwrap ribbon and feathers for trimming
Colouring pencils
Small lid painted gold, eg a toothpaste tube lid

Method

1. Squeeze the top of each tube together and cut away a triangle at the sides 2.5 cm (1 in) wide and 2.5 cm (1 in) deep for the armholes. Cut a 14 cm (5½ in) square of fabric and wrap around the tube. Use fabric glue to stick the fabric to the tube at the back. Glue the lower edge inside the tube, then trim away fabric around the top edge and armholes.

2. Cut out a 15 × 9 cm (6 × 3½ in) rectangle of the same fabric for the sleeves for each king. Use fabric glue sparingly to glue under the short ends. Fold the sleeves in half lengthways with the right side outside. Glue together along the long edges. Trim the pipe-cleaners to 15 cm (6 in) long and insert through the sleeves for arms. Place the arms across the armholes and staple the top edges of each body together.

3. Cut out three 10 × 3.5 cm (4 × 1³/₈ in) strips of pink card for the heads. Overlap the ends by 1.5 cm (⁵/₈ in) and staple together. Place the heads on the bodies and dab household glue inside on the 'shoulders' to attach the heads. Bend the arms forward. Cut out three pairs of hands (template on page 76) from pink card and stick to the ends of the arms with household glue.

4. Cut out three rectangles of fabric for the cloaks 20 × 13 cm (8 × 5 in). Use fabric glue to stick under narrow hems on one long and two short edges. Turn under the top raw edge and gather with running stitches. Wrap the

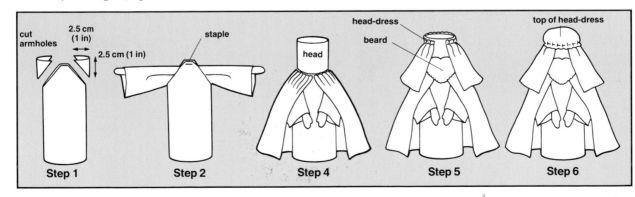

Step 1   cut armholes   2.5 cm (1 in)   2.5 cm (1 in)

Step 2   staple

Step 4   head

Step 5   head-dress   beard

Step 6   top of head-dress

cloak around the body and pull up the gathers under the head. Fasten the upper edges together securely.

5. Cut out a beard (template on page 76) for each king and stick it around the lower edge of each head with fabric glue. Cut out three rectangles of fabric for the head-dresses 12 × 7.5 cm (4¾ × 3 in). Glue under narrow hems on one long and two short edges with fabric glue. Gather the upper raw edge to 7.5 cm (3 in) and wrap around the head with the top edges level and a gap at the front for the face. Glue in place along the gathering.

6. Cut out three circles of fabric with a 6.5 cm (2½ in) diameter for the top of the head-dresses. Gather the circumference, then fill the head with toy filling (wadding), allowing it to stick up above the head. Place the circle on top and pull up the gathers to fit around the head. Dab fabric glue under the gathers to secure in place.

7. Cut out a crown (templates on page 76) for each king from gold card. Wrap around the head and stick the ends together with household glue. Stick on beads, feathers and ribbon for decoration. Carefully cut out three noses (template on page 76) from pink card and stick to the faces with household glue. Draw eyes and eyebrows and rouge the cheeks with colouring pencils.

8. Cut out a 7 cm (2¾ in) square of fabric for one gift. Wrap around a small ball of toy filling (wadding) and tie with gold cord. To make a tub of 'gold', glue a small ball of toy filling (wadding) in the lid. Dab generously with household glue and spread small gold beads on top. For the last gift, glue a small bead on top of a larger one. Glue the gifts between the kings' hands to complete the Magi.

Stained-glass wall hanging

This highly original wall decoration is a luxurious patchwork of dazzling silks and a touch of lurex, which will glow in candlelight. The addition of narrow black bias binding creates the effect of a stained-glass window.

Requirements

Two 30 × 42 cm (12 × 16½ in) pieces of firm silk, calico or cotton, one to be the base fabric and the other, the lining
Scraps of brightly-coloured silk (or cotton fabrics)
Lurex for the candle
Silk or cotton thread for tacking (it is best to use silk thread for sewing silk); black cotton sewing thread
45 cm (½ yd) of 114 cm (45 in) wide black or dark grey cotton lawn
A white pencil
A piece of 60 g (2 oz) polyester wadding 30 × 42 cm (12 × 16½ in) – required only if patchwork is quilted
A 29 × 4 cm (11½ × 1½ in) piece of fabric for a sleeve, in which to insert a length of dowel to hang the patchwork
Two 31 cm (12 in) and two 43 cm (17 in) strips of 2.5 cm (1 in) wide black cotton fabric for the bindings

Method

1. Make individual templates for each pattern piece from page 78 and label with a letter corresponding to the labelling of the pattern pieces on the diagram.
2. Place the templates on the right sides of the fabrics. Pin in place, then draw round the perimeters of the templates in pencil (not pen) and cut out on the pencil line. Leave the templates pinned to the fabric pieces.
3. Fold the base fabric lengthways and gently press to give a centre guideline. Select the fabric pieces for the 'glass' border, remove the templates and pin the fabric pieces in place on the base fabric, butting the edges together but not overlapping them. When you are confident that the pieces are straight, tack them to the base fabric close to the edge

of each piece following the guide to tacking marked on the template on page 78. Gently press the reverse of the work.
4. Centre the candle pieces, pin, then tack in position.
5. To make the 'lead', fold the piece of black or grey cotton lawn in half diagonally and press (see the diagram). Open out the fabric and rule lines at 2.2 cm (⁷⁄₈ in) intervals either side of the diagonal with the white pencil. You will need 5.5 m (18 ft) of strips.
6. Fold the long edges of each strip into the centre to meet (see the diagram). Press well with a steam iron.
7. Following the numerical order marked on the diagram, pin a couple of the strips to the patchwork at a time, with the folded side down and making sure that the 'lead' is centred over the line along which the pieces of fabric butt

together. Sew the 'lead' in place, stitching the inner edge first, using black thread and a straight slip stitch (not slanting) so that the stitches are barely visible. Continue sewing the 'lead' in place, covering up the ends of the short lengths with longer pieces until you have completed the last strip. If you sew a piece of 'lead' in the wrong order, you can easily unpick the edges of the adjoining strip and tuck the 'lead' under. Remove the tacking and press the reverse of the patchwork.

8. If you wish to quilt your panel, cut a piece of 60 g (2 oz) polyester wadding to the size of the base fabric, sandwich it between the patchwork and the lining and secure with tacking stitches. Outline quilting will work well. If you are not quilting, place the lining on the back.

9. Turn under the short edges of the fabric strip for the sleeve and machine stitch. Line up one long edge with the top edge of the lining. Tack all round the edges of the patchwork from the back to hold the lining (and the top of the fabric for the sleeve) in place.

10. Place the two shorter bindings along the top and bottom edges of the patchwork, right sides facing. Pin and machine stitch with a 6 mm (¼ in) seam allowance. Finger press upwards. Sew on the remaining bindings.

11. Turn under the seam allowance on the second long edge of each of the bindings. Slip stitch to the lining (and sleeve) taking care not to let your stitches show on the front.

12. Turn under 6 mm (¼ in) along the bottom edge of the sleeve, and slip stitch to the lining.

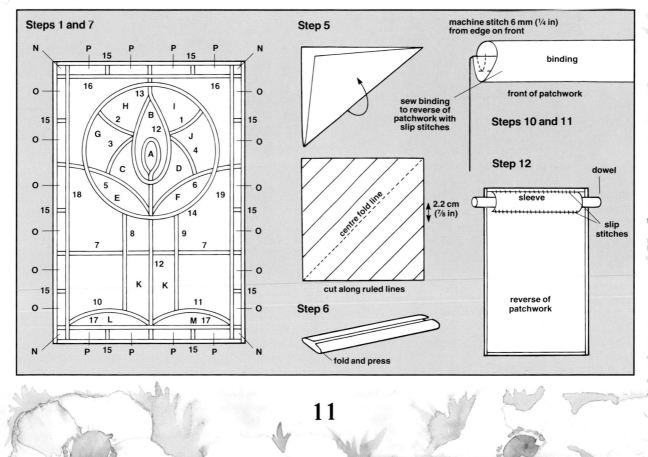

Straw plait with herbs

This tartan trimmed straw plait is not only a visual delight but will fill the room with the heady scent of a kitchen garden as well as provide a ready source of fresh and naturally dried herbs for culinary use. Fresh bunches of herbs can be added when necessary and available.

Requirements

4.5 m (5 yd) of 3 cm (1¼ in) wide tartan ribbon
A florist straw plait
Household glue
Florist reel wire
A selection of different kinds of nuts in the shell
Cinnamon sticks
Star anise
*A selection of fresh culinary herbs: rosemary, sage,
    parsley, marjoram, basil and fennel*
Elastic bands
Florist stub wires

Method

1. Cut two 46 cm (18 in) lengths of ribbon, form two loops and glue one at each end of the plaited portion of the straw. This will enable the plait to be hung if desired.
2. To make the large tartan bows for each end of the plait, take 1.8 m (2 yd) of ribbon and fasten a length of wire around it 10 cm (4 in) from one end. This will form the first 'tail' of one bow and the binding point.
3. Next, form a 4 cm (1½ in) loop and bind to the same place with the wire. Continue to make different-sized loops from the remaining length of ribbon, binding each one tightly with wire, to create one generous bow. Leave a 15 cm (6 in) tail and trim this and the first tail into a 'V'.
4. Repeat steps 2 and 3 with the remaining 1.8 m (2 yd) of ribbon to make the second bow. Glue one bow at each end of the plaited section of the straw.
5. Glue an attractive arrangement of nuts and spices to the centre of the plait.
6. Take individual bunches of herbs, cut the stems short and bind with elastic bands.
7. Twist florist stub wires around the elastic bands leaving a 5 cm (2 in) 'leg' to push into the straw plait.
8. Arrange the herbs along the length of the plait.

Foliage garland

Garlands can be spectacular decorative items, adorning a wall or mantlepiece, door or window.

Requirements

Mixed foliage, eg pine, holly and ivy
Florist reel wire
Florist stub wires
A florist foam garland base
Dried poppy seedheads
Transparent household glue
Gold glitter
Dried gypsophila (baby's breath)
5.5 m (6 yd) of 7.5 cm (3 in) wide white ribbon

Method

1. Cut foliage into short pieces and wire together to form bunches. Use the stub wires to make two 5 cm (2 in) wire 'legs' for each bunch.
2. Push the legs into the garland base and create an even, mixed foliage base.
3. Dab the poppy seedheads with glue and dip them into gold glitter. Wind stub wires around the seedhead stems leaving wire 'legs' to push into the garland.
4. Wire together pieces of gypsophila into bunches and attach stub wires as above.
5. Cut the ribbon into several lengths and wire into bow loops and 'tails'. Position them, using stub wires, on the garland to form a generous bow at the top. Intersperse the bow loops with some poppy seedheads.
6. Add the gypsophila bunches and the remainder of the poppy seedheads, distributing them evenly around the garland to create highlights.

Requirements
30 cm (¹/₃ yd) of 90 cm (36 in)
    wide white satin
A medium-soft pencil
Fine wire (fuse wire)
A pair of pliers
Toy filling or
    polyester wadding
20 cm (8 in) square of firm
    sew-in interfacing
Small gold beads
A beading needle
Small gold sequins

Dove of peace

Method

1. Cut out two 25 cm (10 in) squares of satin and draw the body outline (template on page 79) in pencil on the wrong side of one square. Pin the squares together with the right sides facing and stitch along the outline leaving a gap for turning through on the upper edge of the body.
2. Cut out the body leaving a 6 mm (¼ in) seam allowance around the circumference. Snip the seam allowance at the curves, trim the corners then turn to the right side. Draw the tail divisions on both sides in pencil.
3. Cut a 25 cm (10 in) length of wire with the pliers. Push the wire up through the underside of the body between the stitches. Stuff the body firmly with toy filling (wadding) around the wire. Slip stitch the opening to close.
4. Cut out two 20 cm (8 in) squares of satin and pin together with the right sides facing. Draw the outline of a pair of wings (template on page 79) on the interfacing and pin to the satin squares. Stitch along the outlines leaving a gap for turning through to the right side.
5. Cut out the wings leaving a 6 mm (¼ in) seam allowance around the circumference. Snip the seam allowance at the curves and trim the corners. Turn to the right side and lightly draw the wing divisions on one side.
6. Cut two 12.5 cm (5 in) lengths of wire using the pliers. Insert each wire into a wing, pushing the ends into the tips for support. Slip stitch the openings to close.
7. To work a solid row of beads along the edges of the tail and wings and along the divisions, attach a length of thread to the pencil line or edge. Thread on five beads, lay the beads along the line and insert the needle back into the fabric after the last bead. Make a small back stitch and insert the needle forward through the last bead. Continue along the line.
8. Sew sequins at random to the tail and wing bases.
9. Rows of sequins are sewn close together to cover the beak. Attach a length of thread to the beak and bring out to the right side. Thread on the first sequin and insert the needle close to the left edge of the sequin. Bring out the needle the same distance again to the left.
10. Thread on the next sequin and make a back stitch, inserting the needle to the left of the first sequin. Bring out the needle the same distance beyond the next sequin. Attach the sequins in rows until the beak is covered.
11. To work the eye, bring the needle up through the eye position and thread on a sequin, then a bead. Insert the needle back through the sequin and out through the eye position on the other side. Pull the thread tight so the bead sits on the sequin. Attach a sequin and bead at the eye position on the other side. Sew the wings to each side of the dove's body.

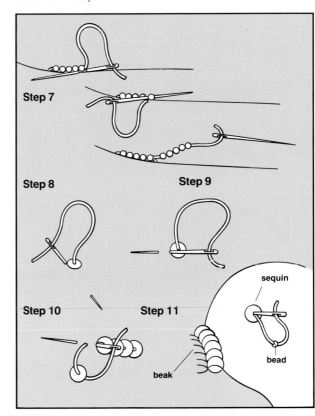

Step 7

Step 8   Step 9

Step 10   Step 11

sequin

beak

bead

Twinkling stars and shimmering butterflies

These glamorous tree decorations are quick, easy and inexpensive to make from transparent PVC. They could also be made out of paper. We used squeeze-bottle writers as an effective but simple way to decorate the fabric.

Requirements
Transparent PVC
A chinagraph pencil
A cutting board
Masking tape
A craft knife with a new blade
A steel ruler
A large cardboard box and newspaper
Spray glue
A selection of lurex fabrics
A pair of sharp scissors
Squeeze-bottle writers in different colours
Adhesive tape
'Toy' antennae or short lengths of pipe-cleaner
Narrow ribbon or decorative string

Method
1. Draw the star and butterfly shapes (templates on pages 73 and 70) onto the PVC using a chinagraph pencil.
2. Lay a double thickness of the PVC on a cutting board and hold in place with masking tape at each corner.
3. Cut out the shapes with the craft knife (and a steel ruler for the stars), applying moderate pressure.
4. Make a spray cabinet by turning a large cardboard box on its side and laying newspaper inside and around the opening. Place the stars and butterflies inside the box. Following the manufacturer's instructions on the can, spray glue the wrong side of the decorations.
5. Press lurex fabric with a cool iron, then stick stars and butterflies onto the fabric. Press with your fingers from the centre outwards to dispel any air bubbles.

HINTS
The stars can be made any size you prefer. They may also be strung across windows, or hung singly or in a group from the ceiling, as a mobile. The butterflies can adorn your house plants, lending them an exotic, festive air.

16

6. Cut out with sharp scissors.

7. Decorate with swirls and squiggles using squeeze-bottle writers. When the liquid comes out of the bottles it is difficult to judge the finished colour, but when dry the colours will be bright and sparkling.

8. Attach the antennae to the butterflies with adhesive tape, and narrow ribbon or decorative string to all the decorations if they are to be hung.

Sequin cubes and balls

Pre-formed polystyrene shapes purchased from craft suppliers can make spectacular tree decorations in just a few simple steps. The balls are divided into four segments with narrow ribbon, then covered with sequins using a different colour for each segment. For the cubes, alternate two complementary colours of sequins on each side.

Requirements
Sequins in a variety of colours
Polystyrene cubes
Polystyrene balls
A pencil
Narrow ribbon in colours to coordinate with the sequins
A packet of short, silver-headed pins

Method
1. Decide on your colour scheme, divide up the sequins into colour groups and put each group of sequins onto a separate saucer.

2. Work out how many sequins you will need for each row on the cubes.

3. Divide up the balls into four segments with a fine pencil line. Pin narrow ribbon in place, leaving a length free for hanging the ornament.

4. Push the pins through the holes in the sequins and into the polystyrene. Build up row after row until the shapes are covered. Pin a length of ribbon to one corner of each cube, to hang.

Gift icicles

'Icicles' filled with sweets make innovative and inviting tree gifts. When the sweets have been eaten, the icicles can be refilled with glitter, tinsel, sequins or tiny pieces of rolled up sweet-papers and then hung on the tree once more. Alternatively, you could present the icicles in a transparent giftbox, like the one in the photograph.

Requirements
A sheet of transparent PVC
A white chinagraph pencil
A cutting board
Masking tape
A steel ruler
Transparent adhesive tape
Sweets or decorative items
Silver and gold glitter pens
Narrow giftwrap ribbon or decorative string

Method
1. Draw the icicles (template on page 71) onto the PVC using the chinagraph pencil.
2. Lay a double thickness of PVC on the cutting board and hold in place with masking tape at each corner. Place the steel ruler along the outside lines and cut out the shapes.
3. Place the fold lines along the edge of a table or worktop and run your thumb and finger along the folds. The fold can be made sharper by running it once more through thumb and finger.
4. When all the folds have been made, punch two holes in each lid. Secure the sides with transparent adhesive tape. You may need another pair of hands to help you.
5. Fill with small sweets or decorative items. Decorate with silver and gold glitter pens if you wish.
6. Thread giftwrap ribbon, which can be curled over scissors, or decorative string through the holes in the lids and close them with narrow pieces of adhesive tape.

> **HINT**
> *Alternatively, you could make some stunning earrings by cutting out smaller icicles, filling them with decorative material and attaching metal earring hooks either through holes pierced in the lids or through the apexes.*

Iced biscuit candles

Simple enough for children to make under close supervision, these tasty biscuits make an eye-catching display hung from the Christmas tree with brightly-coloured ribbon. The quantities given opposite will make approximately 25 biscuits.

Ingredients

85 g (3 oz or 6 tablespoons) butter
85 g (3 oz or 6 tablespoons) sugar
15 ml (1 rounded tablespoon) golden syrup
1 large egg
340 g (12 oz or 3 cups) self-raising flour (or all-purpose
    flour with 3 teaspoons of baking powder)
2.5 ml ($^1/_2$ teaspoon) ground cinnamon
10 ml (2 teaspoons) ground ginger
Icing sugar
Yellow food colouring

Method

1. Cream butter, sugar and golden syrup, then beat in the egg.

2. Sieve in the flour, cinnamon and ginger. Work into a firm dough.

3. Allow the dough to rest for half an hour, then divide into two and roll out each part into fairly thin sheets.

4. Trace out the candle template from page 73 and transfer to thick card. Cut out with scissors or a craft knife (do *not* allow children to use the latter). Use the card template and the point of a sharp kitchen knife (again, adults only) to cut the pastry into candle shapes, remembering to cut out the centre of each 'flame'.

5. With a palette knife, lift the pastry cut-outs from the pastry board onto a lightly-buttered baking sheet and bake for 12 to 15 minutes in an oven pre-heated to 160 °C (325 °F or Gas 3). Allow to cool on a wire tray.

6. Add enough warm water to the icing sugar to make a glacé icing stiff enough to coat the back of a wooden spoon thickly.

7. Lay out the biscuits on sheets of greaseproof (waxed) paper.

8. Coat the candle part only with the icing, noting that the candle slopes at the shoulder.

9. Having iced all the candle 'stems', add a little yellow food colouring to the remaining icing and coat the 'flame' part of each candle, again finishing at an angle at the candle neck. Leave to dry.

19

CHAPTER 2

Natural Gifts

In this section, we have balanced decoration with practicality in a range of hand-crafted gifts inspired by the sights and smells of the countryside and the cottage garden.
Specially conceived with both nature-lovers and the environmentally-aware in mind, these projects use natural materials and ingredients. They also employ a variety of more unusual craft techniques, which you may not have tried before: machine appliqué, salt dough modelling and painting, pressed and dried flower arranging and creating fragrances, lotions and pot-pourri.

21

Hat box

A hat box is both a stylish accessory for the home and a useful, lightweight and attractive storage container, not necessarily for hats but for any keepsakes, for example letters and photographs. Choose a giftwrap paper to make a box that will complement the recipient's home decor.

> **HINTS**
> *Always use a CFC-free spray glue. Preferably use a spray cabinet (see page 16). If paper is stuck in the wrong position with spray glue, it can be lifted and replaced correctly.*

Requirements
A compass
Thick card
Two sheets of black paper
Spray glue
Two sheets of giftwrap paper
Thin card
Transparent adhesive tape
A craft knife

Method
1. Use a compass to draw a circle with a 15 cm (6 in) radius onto thick card for the base. Cut out the base and apply it to black paper with spray glue. Trim away the paper around the circumference, then use the base as a

pattern to cut out one in giftwrap paper.

2. Cut a 1 m × 20 cm (39 × 8 in) strip of thin card for the side of the box. If the card you have is not long enough, cut two 51 × 20 cm (20 × 8 in) strips, overlap the ends by 2.5 cm (1 in) and stick them together with adhesive tape.

3. Place the base on a flat surface. Bend the box side gently to curve it, then wrap it around the base overlapping the ends. Stick the ends together with adhesive tape.

4. To cover the box side, cut two 50 × 23.5 cm (20 × 9¼ in) rectangles of giftwrap paper. Butt them together end to end. Apply adhesive tape on the back over the join.

5. Spray the back of the giftwrap paper heavily with spray glue, then wrap it around the box side with 1.5 cm (⅝ in) extending beyond the top and bottom. Turn the upper edge of the giftwrap to the inside of the box and press in place.

6. Turn the box side upside down and snip into the giftwrap at 1 cm (⅜ in) intervals all around the box. Place the base inside the box with the uncovered side uppermost. Holding the base level with the bottom edge of the box side, stick the snipped edges down onto the base. Use spray glue to apply the giftwrap base to the base of the box covering the snipped edges.

7. To line the box, cut two 50 × 19.5 cm (20 × 7¾ in) strips of black paper. Spray the back of one lining with spray glue, then stick the piece inside the box, carefully butting the lower edge against the base. Stick the other lining inside to cover the opposite side of the box.

8. Cut a circle of thick card with a 15.4 cm (6¹⁄₁₆ in) radius for the lid. Apply the lid to black paper with spray glue, then trim away the paper around the edge.

9. Cut a 1 m × 4 cm (39 × 1½ in) strip of thin card for the band. If the card needs to be joined, cut two 51 × 4 cm (20 × 1½ in) lengths and overlap the ends by 2.5 cm (1 in). Stick the ends together with adhesive tape.

10. Place the lid on a flat surface. Pull the band smoothly between your thumb and a finger to curve it, then wrap the band around the lid. Overlap the ends and stick in place.

11. To cover the lid, cut a circle of giftwrap paper with a radius of 17 cm (6¾ in). Spray the back heavily with spray glue and place the uncovered side of the lid centrally on the sprayed side. Snip into the giftwrap at 1 cm (⅜ in) intervals all round the circumference.

12. Lay the lid black side up on a flat surface and place the band around the circumference. Lift up the snipped edges and stick to the band.

13. Cut two 51 × 5.5 cm (20 × 2¼ in) strips of giftwrap paper. Butt the strips end to end and apply adhesive tape on the back over the join. Spray the back heavily with spray glue and wrap the strip around the band with the excess extending beyond the lower edge. Turn the lower edge of the giftwrap to the inside of the box and press.

14. Cut two 51 × 3.5 cm (20 × 1¼ in) strips of black paper to line the band. Spray the back of the strips with spray glue and stick inside the band, butting the long edge against the base.

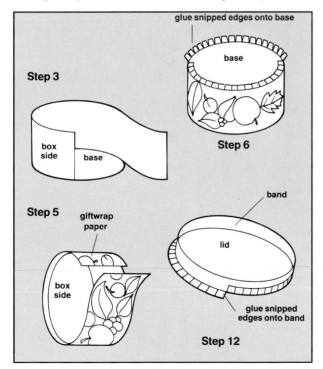

glue snipped edges onto base

base

Step 3

box side   base

Step 6

band

lid

Step 5

giftwrap paper

box side

glue snipped edges onto band

Step 12

Victorian 'scrap' cushions

These Victorian-style cushions are shaped to resemble a fire-screen. The Victorians cut out scraps of fabric, applied them in an elaborate arrangement to fire-screens, then coated them with varnish. Here we have cut flowers and foliage from a variety of fabrics to make a collage of blooms. Use offcuts or soft-furnishing sample books, often on sale when the new season's collections are launched.

Requirements

One 41 × 35.5 cm (16 × 14 in) piece of paper and one 33 × 25.5 cm (13 × 10 in)
70 cm (³/₄ yd) of 115 cm (45 in) wide green fabric
A selection of floral fabrics
Pins
Bonding web
A piece of scrap cloth
Machine embroidery threads for satin stitching
'Tear-away' paper or typing paper
Two 23 cm (9 in) zips and one 33 cm (13 in) zip
70 cm (³/₄ yd) of 115 cm (45 in) wide fabric for inner cushions
Cushion filling
For the piping, if used:
2.5 m (2³/₄ yd) of 3 cm (1¹/₄ in) wide bias binding
2.5 m (2³/₄ yd) narrow (no 2) piping cord

Method

1. Fold the pieces of paper in half lengthways and cut a curve at one end of each piece through both thicknesses of paper. Open out pattern pieces.
2. Using the pattern pieces, cut three cushion fronts (two small and one large) from the green fabric.
3. Cut out flowers from your selection of fabrics just outside the perimeter. Arrange them on the green fabric.
4. Pin the flowers right side down onto the paper side of bonding web. Cut out as accurately as possible, otherwise the web will stick to the iron. Remove pins and separate the fabric pieces from the bonding web, but keep in pairs.

5. Cover the ironing board with a piece of clean, scrap cloth to prevent the flowers sticking to the board. Lay the flowers right side down and carefully position the corresponding pieces of bonding web, rough (glue) side down, on top of the flowers. Press with a steam iron. When all the flowers are bonded, tear off the paper backing and arrange the flowers on the green fabric.
6. Press gently with the iron to attach the flowers to the green fabric. Leave to cool, then carefully turn the fabric

over and press again on the reverse.

7. Put a new medium-fine needle in the sewing machine and set the machine to a close zig-zag stitch. Use an embroidery foot if your machine has one. Satin stitch the outside edge of each flower to the green fabric. Work a sample piece first to check your stitching and technique. Leave the start and finish threads hanging while you work. When you have completed the panel, pull the threads through to the back of the fabric and knot. You may find it easier to keep the stitches even if you place a piece of typing paper or purpose-made paper underneath the fabric when machine stitching. Gently tear the paper away from the stitches when you have finished and press the panel. Complete the remaining panels in the same way.

8. Cut the cushion backs from the green fabric, making each of them 6.5 cm (2½ in) longer than the pattern. Cut each back in half widthways, fold under a narrow seam allowance on the top edge of the lower half and position the zip underneath the seam so that the fabric covers half the width of the zip (see the diagram). Machine stitch this half of the zip to the cushion back. Making sure the back is the same length as the front, fold under a seam allowance along the bottom edge of the top half of the cushion back. Place this edge so that it covers the other half of the zip and stitch in place.

9. If you want to sew piping round the cushions to help them keep in shape, cut a strip of bias binding to fit round the top and sides of the cushion (there is no need to pipe the base). Fold the bias binding in half around the piping cord (cut to the same length as the bias binding). Tack the long edges together or machine stitch, using the zipper foot, close to the cord.

10. Matching rough edges, pin, then tack the piping to the perimeter of the cushion on the right side.

11. Pin cushion backs to cushion fronts with right sides facing. Open the zips and machine stitch around the outside edges. If you have opted for the piping, use a zipper foot and stitch as close to the piping as you can.

12. Snip up to the stitching line around the arched portion of each cushion, trim off the corners diagonally and turn

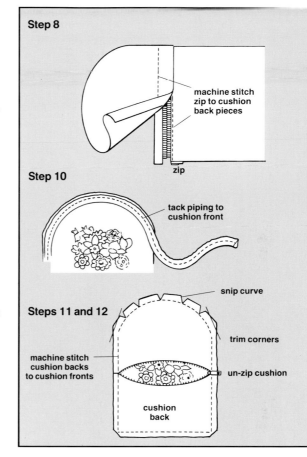

through to the right side. Press well.

13. To make the inner cushions, cut four pieces from the fabric using the small pattern, and two pieces using the larger pattern. Match the two sides for each cushion and machine stitch around the outer edges, leaving a small gap for turning through. Snip the arched edges, trim the corners diagonally and turn through. Stuff with filling until plump, then machine or hand stitch the opening closed. Place inner cushions inside the cushion covers and zip up.

Fruity wall plaque

If you enjoy making pastry, salt dough is an ideal medium for you to work with. Cheap and easy to produce, the ingredients for the dough are probably already in the kitchen cupboard. The dough is baked slowly in a domestic oven and can then be painted when it has cooled. Water-colour paints give a gentle, natural effect that is ideally suited to the rustic quality of the basket of luscious fruit.

Requirements
225 g (8 oz or 2 cups) plain (all-purpose) flour
225 g (8 oz or 2 cups) salt
280 ml (10 fl oz or 1¼ cups) water
A rolling pin
An old, blunt craft knife blade for cutting
A paperclip
A pair of pliers
Water-colour paints and brushes
Clear, matt varnish

Method

1. Mix together the flour, salt and water. Turn out the mixture and knead until you have a pliable dough. Keep dough not in use in an airtight container.

2. Roll out a piece of dough to 6 mm (¼ in) thick and cut out the base (template on page 74). Indent the basket line. To make the basket, roll out the dough to 3 mm (⅛ in) thick and cut 1 cm (⅜ in) wide strips. Arrange short lengths vertically side by side on the lower half of the base. Carefully weave longer lengths horizontally through the vertical strips. Cut off the ends level with the basket line and outer edges.

3. Roll four sausages of dough approximately 1 cm (⅜ in) thick and twist together in pairs. Moisten and place against the top and lower edges of the basket.

4. Roll dough out flat 6 mm (¼ in) thick and cut out a vine leaf and a cherry leaf (templates on page 74). Indent the veins. Roll nine 2 cm (¾ in) diameter balls of dough for the grapes. Mould into ovals.

5. To make the pear, roll a 4.5 cm (1¾ in) diameter ball of dough. Squeeze one side to mould into a pear shape and then flatten slightly. Roll two 3 cm (1¼ in) diameter balls of dough for the apple and orange. Flatten both slightly and dent the top of the apple. Make a hole near the top of the orange.

6. Moisten the top half of the base and arrange the vine leaf and fruits in position.

7. Roll a 3 cm (1¼ in) diameter ball of dough. Mould into an oval for the plum. Roll a 3.5 cm (1½ in) diameter ball of dough for the peach. Flatten slightly and cut off the lower third. Pat the cut edges to curve them. Make a deep dent in the top of the plum and the peach.

8. Roll two 2 cm (¾ in) diameter balls of dough for the cherries. Arrange the remaining fruit and cherry leaf on the plaque. Roll a thin sausage of dough for stalks and extend between the cherries and the leaf. Cut off a short length and press to the top of the pear.

9. Snip the rounded ends off the paperclip with a pair of pliers and press the ends into the top of the base on the back so that the plaque can be hung on a wall.

10. Bake the plaque in a domestic oven at 120 °C (250 °F or Gas ½) for 2¼ hours.

11. When the plaque has cooled after baking, paint the basket and fruit with water-colour paints. Varnish the plaque all over six times, allowing the varnish to dry completely between coats.

Lavender moisturizing cream

Moisturizers are vitally important in maintaining the skin's natural moisture. Additionally, lavender has always been valued for its great healing properties. This cream is wonderfully light, quickly absorbed by the skin and mildly fragrant.

Ingredients

425 ml (¾ pint or 2 cups) boiling water
60 g (2 oz or 2 cups) lavender flowers
Coffee filter paper
5 ml (1 teaspoon) beeswax
10 ml (2 teaspoons) lanolin
40 ml (8 teaspoons) almond oil
A pinch of borax
Screw-top jars

Method

1. Make an infusion by pouring the boiling water over the lavender flowers.

2. Cover and leave for 30 minutes.

3. Strain the infusion through coffee filter paper.

4. Melt the wax in an enamel double boiler, then beat in the lanolin and oil.

5. Add a pinch of borax to the strained infusion and reheat without boiling.

6. Remove the wax mixture from the heat and slowly whisk in the infusion.

7. Continue to beat the mixture until a smooth cream is achieved.

8. Beat the mixture until it cools, then scoop into jars.

Christmas splash

This is a fresh, tangy cologne for men – a traditional gift made extra special by the personal touch.

Ingredients
A handful of bay leaves
A handful of sweet basil
A handful of pine needles
A handful of rosemary
15 ml (3 teaspoons) grated lemon rind
15 ml (3 teaspoons) grated orange rind
A pestle and mortar
10 ml (2 teaspoons) whole cloves
1 stick cinnamon
A screw-top jar
280 ml (10 fl oz or 1¼ cups) ethyl alcohol or vodka
Coffee filter paper
Dark bottles

Method
1. Wash and dry the herbs, chop into a bowl and add the grated rind.
2. Using the pestle and mortar, pound together the cloves and cinnamon.
3. Add the ground cloves and cinnamon to the other ingredients and mix together thoroughly.
4. Pack into a screw-top jar and pour on the alcohol or vodka.
5. Secure the lid and shake daily for two weeks.
6. Strain the mixture through a coffee filter paper into dark bottles.
7. Secure bottle tops or stoppers tightly. Place in a dark cupboard to mature for at least six weeks.

Rosemary and lavender bath oils

Pamper your loved ones with luxurious, skin-softening baths for weeks to come by making them a gift of these natural, fragrant oils. A little of the oil poured under a fast-running bath tap will create foaming, aromatic water.

Ingredients
Rosemary oil:
25 ml (5 teaspoons) rosemary essential oil
225 ml (8 fl oz) almond oil (or sunflower oil as a cheaper alternative)
25 ml (5 teaspoons) plain mild shampoo
25 ml (5 teaspoons) vodka or Polish spirit
Lavender oil:
25 ml (5 teaspoons) lavender essential oil
225 ml (8 fl oz) almond oil (or sunflower oil as a cheaper alternative)
25 ml (5 teaspoons) plain mild shampoo
25 ml (5 teaspoons) vodka or Polish spirit
1 drop red vegetable food colouring
Stoppered or screw-top bottles

28

Method

Simply put all the ingredients together for each bath oil into two separate tall bottles with stoppers or screw tops and shake well. They will mix together to form a creamy emulsion. Shake again before use.

Rosemary and lavender bath vinegars

Rosemary vinegar:
570 ml (20 fl oz or 2^1/$_2$ cups) cider vinegar
Five rosemary sprigs
15 ml (1 tablespoon) fresh thyme leaves
Lavender vinegar:
570 ml (20 fl oz or 2^1/$_2$ cups) cider vinegar
Fifteen lavender stems
Wide-necked, screw-top jars
Stoppered bottles

Method
1. Bring the vinegar to the boil in a stainless steel or enamel saucepan (not aluminium) and add the herbs. Take off the heat and replace the lid.
2. Allow to cool slightly and pour into the jars.
3. After a week, strain the vinegars into two separate bottles.

A basketful of pot-pourri

The soft blue-grey of the dried lavender combines subtly and beautifully with the deep, dark pink of the dried roses in this everlasting arrangement. Additionally, the basket will bring a hint of fresh, country fragrance into the home.

Requirements
A small, shallow basket with a handle
A sheet of plastic to line the basket
Soft florist clay
Dried roses with stems and rosebuds
Dried lavender stems
Household glue
60 g (2 oz or 2 cups) dried lavender flowers
115 g (4 oz or 1 cup) dried rose petals
30 ml (2 tablespoons) powdered orris root

Method
1. Line the basket with a layer of plastic.
2. Secure a ball of clay to the inside rim of the basket where the handle joins.
3. Arrange roses and lavender against the basket handle, setting the stems in the clay.
4. Glue a pleasing arrangement of rosebuds and short lavender stems to the front of the basket.
5. Blend the dried rose petals and lavender flowers with the orris root and fill the basket.

Pressed flower photograph mount

This delicate and subtly-coloured pressed flower design has been specifically conceived not to overpower but complement the photograph it frames. A hand-crafted mount will elevate the gift of a family portrait or a period picture to heirloom status.

Requirements
Mounting board
A ready-made wooden picture frame
A craft knife
Pressed maidenhair fern (Adiantum pedatum), *fuchsia, potentilla, hydrangea, feverfew* (Matricaria eximia), *hedge parsley* (Torilis japonica)
Rubber-based glue (contact adhesive)
A cocktail stick or toothpick
A pair of stamp tweezers and a paintbrush
Masking tape

Method
1. Cut a piece of mounting board to fit the frame. Allowing a wide margin for the pressed flower design, cut an aperture and position the mount over the photograph.
2. Break the fern into small pieces and apply rubber-based glue (contact adhesive) with a cocktail stick or toothpick,

Using the tweezers, position the fern pieces on the mount to form the outline of the design.

3. Position a long spray of potentilla in the centre of the 'outline'. Group the hydrangea throughout the fern 'outline'. Build up the design with potentilla and feverfew, allowing the pointed hydrangea petals to contrast to best effect with the rounded petals of the potentilla flowers.

4. Position the fuchsia to break up the solidity of the design, then add hedge parsley throughout to highlight.

5. Dust the mount using a paintbrush. Clean the glass thoroughly and place over the mount. Lower the frame over the glass. Hold the frame, glass and mount together firmly and turn over. Fit the picture frame back securely and seal the edges with masking tape.

CHAPTER 3

Table Gifts

At Christmas time, we can feel free to savour those little indulgences without the nagging feelings of guilt, and our minds naturally turn to titivating the taste-buds. You can be confident that food-fanciers everywhere will greatly appreciate a gift of hand-made luxury sweetmeats or savouries. The recipes we have chosen use easily-obtainable ingredients and are delightfully simple to follow. But the results are sumptuous! Some are quick to achieve – ideal for last-minute gifts.

We have also included projects for seasonal tableware and table decorations, to enhance the festive feasting.

Golden glow centrepiece

A sumptuous table centrepiece, fit to adorn even the grandest of festive feasts. Use any combination of interestingly shaped or textured dried plant material.

Ingredients

A florist plastic pinholder (a four-pronged anchor for holding the block of foam)
A circular or rush cork mat
A fixative for securing the plastic pinholder to the mat
A block of dry foam
Two plastic candle-holders
A large cardboard box
Gold spray paint
A selection of plant material: dried, pressed or silk fern leaves; dried poppy seedheads; dried barley and ornamental grasses; cones; ivy
Approximately 75 cm (29 in) of 5 cm (2 in) wide wired ribbon
Florist stub wires
Florist black reel wire
Household glue
Two gold candles

Method

1. Secure the plastic pinholder to the centre of the mat using the special fixative. Impale the block of foam on the pinholder's prongs and mount the plastic candle-holders.
2. Place the mat in a large cardboard box placed on its side on newspaper. Spray with gold paint.
3. Place a few of the plant items in the box at a time. Spray with paint, turning to coat evenly.
4. Bend ribbon into loops and secure with black reel wire. Wind a stub wire around the base of each loop to make two 5 cm (2 in) 'legs' with which to mount the ribbon onto the foam. Wire two ribbon 'tails' in the same way.
5. Wind black reel wire around the cones, leaving 'legs' to mount them onto the foam, or glue stub wire onto their bases. Group the grasses into small bunches and secure

with wire, again leaving 'legs' for mounting.
6. Shorten one of the candles by approximately 2.5 cm (1 in). Place the candles in the candle-holders.
7. Use the fern leaves to create the basic 'architecture' of your arrangement. Group the bow loops and 'tails' to form a focal point. Intersperse cones, grasses, ivy and seedheads to fill the block of foam and complete the arrangement.

Vine-stencilled wine glasses

Enhance a set of plain wine glasses with a rich design of vines and grapes stencilled in gold. To stencil onto glass, you will need a paint specially formulated for ceramic or glass so that the design will withstand repeated handling and washing. Good art and craft shops have a selection which are air-drying. Make sure the glasses are straight-sided so that the stencil will lie flat.

Requirements

Stencil board
Tracing paper
Carbon paper
Masking tape
A craft knife
Straight-sided wine glasses; we chose some of Spanish origin made from re-cycled glass
Gold ceramic paint
A stencil brush
A ceramic tile or an old plate
An old paintbrush

Method

1. To transfer the design to the stencil board, trace the template on page 70 onto the tracing paper, then place carbon paper ink-side down on the stencil board. Stick the tracing on top with masking tape. Re-draw the design to transfer the motif to the board.

2. Remove the carbon and tracing paper. Carefully cut out the sections of the stencil with a craft knife, then cut round the stencil leaving a 1.5 cm (⅝ in) wide margin around the edges.

3. Tape the stencil onto one of the glasses. Mark the position of the rim on the stencil board so that the stencil can be placed in the same position on the other glasses.

4. It is most important when stencilling to pick up only a small amount of paint on the stencil brush. A simple way to achieve this is to first paint a thin layer of paint on a smooth, flat surface, such as a ceramic tile or an old plate,

using an old paintbrush.

5. Dab at the painted surface with the stencil brush held upright. Now dab the brush through the cut-outs, moving the brush in a circular motion to distribute the paint evenly. Leave to dry before applying a second coat.

6. When the design is completely dry, remove the stencil board. Any smudges can be removed with white spirit.

Log Cabin table-mats and coasters

Log Cabin is a traditional patchwork design, developed by the North American settlers along with Cathedral Window, Rose of Sharon and many more designs. The centre square is in red or sometimes black fabric, symbolizing the fire or hearth of the cabin; the strips of fabric denote the logs of the cabin walls.

The use of a dark-coloured fabric on one half of the patchwork and a light-coloured fabric on the other offers an additional overall design element when separate patchwork pieces are placed or joined together. Here we have formed a dark (or light) diamond by placing the four patchwork pieces together, making an attractive centre-piece for the dining table when not in use. Separated, they can then fulfil their practical function as table-mats.

Requirements

For the table-mats:
60 cm (24 in) of 114 cm (45 in) wide dark-coloured fabric
60 cm (24 in) of 114 cm (45 in) wide light-coloured fabric
Four 4 cm (1½ in) squares of gold fabric
Four 28 cm (11 in) squares of base calico
Four 28 cm (11 in) squares of 60 g (2 oz) polyester wadding

Method

1. Press all the fabrics thoroughly, since you will not be able to do so once the wadding is in place.
2. It is important to work as accurately as possible to ensure that the finished mats are all the same size. Check the straight of grain of the dark and light fabrics and press the edges. Measure six strips 3 cm (1¼ in) wide across the width of each piece of fabric and cut. Then measure and cut two 28 cm (11 in) squares from each remaining piece of fabric for the linings.
3. Fold each calico square in half diagonally and gently press. Open and fold along the second diagonal, then press. Pin wadding to the reverse of each calico square and tack along the press lines. This will be your guide for placing and sewing the fabric strips.
4. Tack a gold fabric square to the centre of the calico, aligning each corner with the tacking lines (see the diagram). The 'logs' will cover the raw edges.
5. Lay a light-coloured fabric strip right side down on top of the gold square matching the top and one short edge. Trim the strip to match the 'length' of the gold square. Pin and machine stitch the 'strip' to the gold square 6 mm (¼ in) from the top edges. Lift up the 'flap' and finger press flat.
6. Turn the mat anti-clockwise (to your left) so that the light-coloured fabric is positioned to the left of the gold square. Lay another light-coloured strip right side down matching the top edges of the sewn fabric pieces. Trim to size, pin and machine stitch the fabric strip to the two squares as described above. Finger press the 'flap' outwards and turn the mat anti-clockwise again.

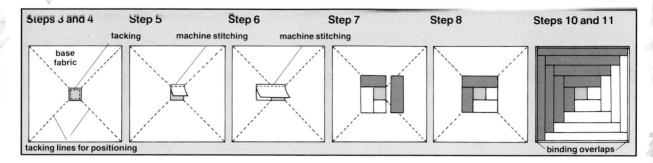

| Steps 3 and 4 | Step 5 | Step 6 | Step 7 | Step 8 | Steps 10 and 11 |

base fabric

tacking

machine stitching

machine stitching

tacking lines for positioning

binding overlaps

HINT

To make a wall hanging, join the table-mats together with hooks and eyes. Slip stitch a fabric sleeve slightly shorter than the full width of the wall hanging across the top of the mat backs, to hold a length of dowel (see page 11).

7. Lay a dark-coloured fabric strip right side down matching the top edges of the gold square and the light-coloured fabric strip. Trim to size, pin and machine stitch as before. Finger press the strip outwards. The left-hand top and bottom corners of the strips should meet the tacking lines. If they do not, un-pick the machine stitching, press the 'log' and re-sew to fit. Complete the centre square of 'logs' with a dark-coloured fabric strip.

8. Continue sewing on the fabric strips in the same way until the patchwork measures 27 cm (10½ in) square. Complete all four mats to the same measure and trim excess calico.

9. Place and pin a lining to the reverse of each mat.

10. To bind the edges, select a light-coloured fabric strip and, with right sides together and matching long edges, pin and machine stitch the binding to the mat with a 6 mm (¼ in) seam allowance. Press the strip outwards. Complete the second light-coloured fabric binding, then the two dark-coloured fabric bindings. Sew the bindings on all four mats in the same order, so that when they are placed or joined together the 'overlaps' match.

11. Slip stitch the bindings to the reverse of the mats, turning under a small seam allowance and folding in the ends of the bindings at the corners.

12. For the matching coasters, cut 13 cm (5 in) squares of base calico, wadding and fabric for the linings; a 2 cm (¾ in) square of gold fabric for the centre of each coaster, and 2.5 cm (1 in) wide strips from the dark and light-coloured fabrics. Follow the instructions given for the table-mats.

Peaches and pears in brandy

The delicate flesh of peaches and pears can be preserved steeped in a subtly-spiced syrup laced with a fine brandy. You will have fun seeking out interesting, old-fashioned bottling jars, in which to pack and present the fruit attractively. Alternatively, you can enhance the more modern variety with a length of decorative ribbon tied in a bow around the top of the jar, as we did.

This is a slow-maturing gift, not to be hurried – the fruit should be left for at least three months before eating – but well worth waiting for.

Ingredients
570 ml (20 fl oz or 2¹/₂ cups) water
225 g (8 oz or 1 cup) sugar
Two cloves
¹/₂ stick cinnamon
Four small peaches, preferably the white-fleshed variety
Four small pears
A tall bottling jar
100 ml (4 fl oz or ³/₄ cup) brandy

Method
1. Put the water into a stainless steel saucepan, add the sugar, cloves and cinnamon, and bring to the boil.
2. Dip the peaches in some boiling water to ease peeling. Peel, halve and stone the peaches.
3. Peel the pears, cut in half and remove the cores with the bowl of a teaspoon.
4. Place the fruit in the boiling syrup, reduce the heat and simmer for 15 minutes.
5. Carefully remove the fruit from the syrup and allow to cool. Remove the cloves and cinnamon from the syrup and return it to the heat to reduce it to one-fifth of its original quantity.
6. Pack the fruit in an attractive arrangement into a tall bottling jar.
7. Add the brandy to the cooled reduced syrup, pour into the jar and seal.

Brandy and almond butter

A new and mouthwatering variation on a traditional theme. Encourage recipients to spread the butter on thin slices of toasted brown bread for a special tea-time treat.

Ingredients
75 g (2¹/₂ oz or ²/₃ cup) ground almonds
115 g (4 oz or a scant cup) icing (confectioner's) sugar
450 g (1 lb or 2 cups) unsalted butter cut into small cubes
100 ml (4 fl oz or ³/₄ cup) brandy
A cork-stoppered or screw-top jar
A small amount of fabric
An elastic band
Ribbon

Method
1. Using a wooden spoon, blend ground almonds, icing sugar and butter in a small mixing bowl.
2. When fully blended, gradually add the brandy a little at a time, whipping into the mixture with a fork or small balloon whisk. The precise amount of brandy that the mixture can take will depend on the amount of water in the butter and the dryness of the ground almonds. If the mixture begins to separate, place the bowl in a cool place for 15 minutes, then add a heaped teaspoon of ground almonds and beat again.
3. Spoon into a cork-stoppered or screw-top jar. Make a cover for the screw-top lid by drawing a circle at least 7.5 cm (3 in) larger in diameter than the lid on the wrong side of a scrap of pretty fabric. Fix the fabric circle over the lid with an elastic band and cover with a colour-coordinated ribbon.

> **HINT**
> *If you choose a smooth-sided cork-stoppered jar, you can decorate it with the wine glass vine stencil (instructions on page 35; template on page 70).*

Rum and chocolate noisettes

These delicious, luxury chocolates will provide a memorable but undoubtedly short-lived treat for family or friends. Present them in petit-four cases packed in a decorative box or a basket enhanced with festive ribbon.

Ingredients
225 g (8 oz or 1¼ cups) plain cooking chocolate
5 ml (1 level teaspoon) cooking oil
60 g (2 oz or ¼ cup) marzipan
85 g (3 oz or ⅔ cup) dried milk powder
60 ml (2 fl oz or ¼ cup) dark rum
60 g (2 oz or ½ cup) chopped almonds
Cocoa powder

Method
1. Melt the chocolate with the oil in a non-stick pan and remove from the heat.
2. Divide the marzipan into small pieces and, using a wooden spoon, blend into the chocolate.
3. Add the powdered milk and mix until the mixture becomes evenly crumbly in texture.
4. Add the rum and beat into a smooth paste.
5. Stir in half the almonds and leave to cool a little.
6. When the mixture is cool enough to hold its shape, take small pieces and roll into balls on a sheet of greaseproof (waxed) paper covered with sifted cocoa powder.
7. Take half of the balls and dip the tops into a saucer containing the remainder of the chopped nuts. Then roll the bottom half of these balls in an equal mixture of cocoa and powdered milk. Set out to harden.

Sweet pepper paté

A rich terrine of paté to tempt the taste buds. Certainly a gift to savour!

Ingredients
450 g (1 lb) pork sausagemeat
225 g (8 oz or ½ lb) minced (ground) pig's liver
115 g (4 oz or ¼ lb) finely chopped streaky pork
Two cloves of garlic, finely chopped
100 ml (4 fl oz or ¾ cup) dry cider
Salt and pepper to taste
One large green and one large red pepper
225 g (8 oz or ½ lb) streaky bacon, with rind removed

Method
1. Mix the sausagemeat, liver, pork, garlic, cider and salt and pepper together and leave to stand for an hour.
2. Cut the peppers into 2.5 cm (1 in) wide strips and blanch in boiling water for one minute and drain.
3. Line a terrine with the slices of streaky bacon in a diagonal arrangement. Put in a 1.2 cm (½ in) layer of

Curried nuts

Some like it hot and these spicy nuts are sure to fulfil their Eastern promise. This is a delightfully simple recipe which gives an original and highly attractive result.

Ingredients
85 g (3 oz or 6 tablespoons) butter
2.5 ml (¹/₂ teaspoon) Madras curry powder
115 g (4 oz or 1 cup) shelled, halved walnuts
115 g (4 oz or 1 cup) shelled, whole almonds
5 ml (1 heaped teaspoon) Tandoori spice mix (ground)
115 g (4 oz or 1 cup) shelled, whole hazelnuts
5 ml (1 heaped teaspoon) Garam Masala spice mix
   (ground)
A transparent giftbox or glass jar

Method
1. Melt the butter in a non-stick pan, add the Madras curry powder and lightly fry the walnuts for two minutes.
2. Take off the heat, add a teaspoon of water and return the pan to the heat until all the water has evaporated. This simple process allows the nuts to absorb the curry flavour to the full.
3. Using a perforated spoon, lift out the nuts into a large sieve. Allow them to drain back into the non-stick pan, then empty the nuts out onto kitchen paper to cool.
4. Repeat the above procedure with the almonds, using the same butter/curry mixture. After draining off the surplus butter and while the almonds are still hot, transfer them to a small bowl containing the Tandoori spice mix. Shake the almonds around the bowl until they are well-coated with spice, then leave to cool. Shake off any surplus spice mix.
5. Prepare the hazelnuts in the same way as the almonds but coat them with Garam Masala spice mix.
6. The three varieties of nuts will each have a distinctive colour as well as flavour and can be displayed to great effect by packing in strips into a transparent box or in layers into a glass jar.

meat mixture, and then a layer of green pepper strips. Cover with a second layer of meat mixture, followed by a layer of red pepper strips. Cover with the remainder of the meat and press down well.
4. Place the terrine in a tray of water and bake for 1 ¹/₂ hours at 160 °C (325 °F or Gas 3).
5. Cool for at least 24 hours under a weighted board.

41

CHAPTER 4

Working Gifts

Many people prefer to give and receive really useful items, as opposed to something entirely frivolous. But purchased practical gifts can often seem predictable, unoriginal and impersonal. However, when these objects are hand-crafted to a unique design with personalized details, they can be transformed into 'designer gifts'.

Here, we have taken some 'old faithful' gift ideas and presented them in a fresh, sophisticated and stylish form. Some are classic and elegant in their design style; others contemporary, bold and abstract.

Herbal coat hanger

Requirements

A wooden coat hanger

7 × 81 cm (3 × 32 in) foam wadding to wrap around the hanger; and 16.5 × 61 cm (6 × 24 in) for the cover

16.5 × 61 cm (6 × 24 in) tartan fabric for the cover; 4 × 15 cm (1½ × 6 in) to cover the hook; 15 × 11.5 cm (6 × 4½ in) for the tie back; 18 × 27 cm (7 × 10½ in) for the front; 9 × 7.5 cm (3½ × 3 in) for the knot

A 16.5 × 61 cm (6 × 24 in) piece of muslin

Mixed ground herbs: cinnamon, cloves, dried wormwood or southernwood leaves, dried rosemary

Method

1. Wrap the wadding around the hanger to pad.

2. Sandwich together the tartan fabric for the cover, wadding and muslin in that order and machine stitch lines at 1.5 cm (½ in) intervals. Fold in half lengthways.

3. Snip the fabric halfway along the length of the fold.

4. Shape the ends of the fabric as shown in the diagram.

5. Fold the quilted fabric in half lengthways with right sides facing. Machine stitch the curved ends of the fabric together with a 1.2 cm (½ in) seam allowance and trim.

6. Turn the cover to the right side and fit over the hanger, inserting the hook through the hole. Trim back the wadding at the base of the hanger, turn under a 1.2 cm (½ in) hem along one long edge of the cover, overlap the other long edge and slip stitch to close.

7. Fold the strip of tartan for the hook in half lengthways and machine stitch a 1.2 cm (½ in) seam along one short edge and along the long edge. Trim close to the stitching and pull the strip through to the right side. Slip over the hook and hand sew to the cover.

8. Fold the tartan fabric for the tie back in half lengthways with right sides facing. Machine stitch a 1.2 cm (½ in) seam around the three sides leaving a small gap. Turn through to the right side.

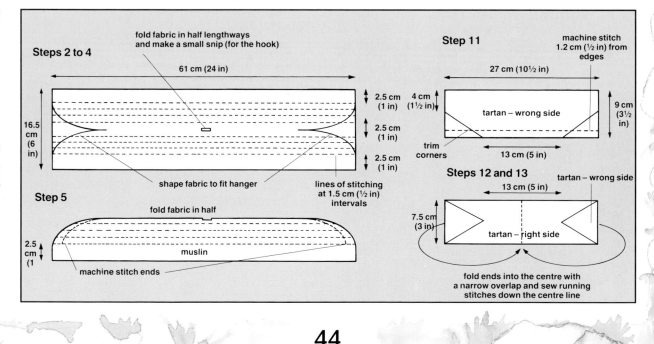

9. Fill with the ground herbs. Close gap with slip stitches.

10. Sew a line of running stitches down the centre (across the width) of the tie back through both thicknesses of fabric. Pull to gather and stitch through to secure.

11. To make the tie front, fold the tartan fabric in half lengthways and machine stitch a 1.2 cm (½ in) seam along the long edge. Trim the corners – see the diagram.

12. Turn the fabric to the right side and position the seam along the centre of the fabric (see the diagram) and press.

13. Fold the short edges of the fabric into the centre with a narrow overlap. Sew a line of running stitches down the centre line through all the thicknesses of fabric. Pull the thread to gather, secure and sew to the tie back.

14. Fold the tartan fabric strip for the knot in half lengthways with right sides facing. Machine stitch a 1.2 cm (½ in) seam down the long edge. Turn to the right side and use to cover the gathered centre of the bow-tie. Sew to close at the back of the bow.

15. Sew the bow-tie to the cover at the base of the hook.

A treat for feet

Requirements
Paper and household glue
45 cm (½ yd) of 112 cm (44 in) wide moiré fabric
20 cm (¼ yd) lightweight wadding
90 cm (1 yd) of 1 cm (⅜ in) wide patterned ribbon
45 cm (½ yd) of 2.3 cm (⅞ in) wide patterned ribbon
45 cm (½ yd) of 90 cm (36 in) wide close weave fabric,
  the same colour as the moiré
30 cm (⅓ yd) of 90 cm (36 in) wide pelmet interfacing
30 cm (⅓ yd) square of 6 mm (¼ in) thick foam

Method
1. Cut out a complete sole pattern (see page 76) in paper. Lengthen or shorten the pattern to fit along the given line. Adjust the sole cover pattern by the same amount.

2. Cut out four uppers to the fold in moiré fabric and two in wadding. Tack narrow ribbon across two uppers 1.3 cm (½ in) below the straight edge. Stitch close to the ribbon edges. Tack wide ribbon below the first row and stitch close to the edges, then another row of narrow ribbon.

3. Tack wadding to the wrong side of the trimmed uppers. Stitch the darts in all the uppers and trim excess wadding.

4. With the right sides facing, stitch each trimmed upper to a plain upper 1 cm (⅜ in) from the straight edges. Trim away excess wadding. Turn to the right side and press. Tack the raw edges together, enclosing the wadding.

5. Cut two sole covers in moiré fabric and two in close weave fabric. With right sides uppermost, tack uppers to moiré sole covers between dots and matching notches.

6. Stitch close weave sole covers on top matching right sides, dots and notches (1 cm/⅜ in seam). Leave a 9 cm (3½ in) gap on a straight edge to turn. Trim away excess wadding and snip curves. Turn to the right side.

7. Cut four soles in interfacing (glue two together per slipper); two in foam. Glue foam soles on top of the interfacing soles.

8. Insert soles into the slippers, foam uppermost, to lie flat. Slip-stitch openings to close.

Marbled stationery case

Filing letters and stationery is made easy and pleasurable with this practical and elegant case. The folder is made from sturdy mounting board covered with marbled paper and has reinforced corners (covered with carpet tape) to make it extra hard-wearing.

Requirements
Mounting board
Two sheets of marbled paper
Spray glue
90 cm (1 yd) of 1.5 cm (⅝ in) wide black ribbon
Strong Glue
One sheet of black leatherette paper
1.3 m (1⅜ yd) of 5 cm (2 in) wide black carpet tape
Double-sided adhesive tape

Method
1. Cut out two 33 × 26 cm (13 × 10¼ in) rectangles of mounting board and two 37 × 28 cm (14½ × 11 in) rectangles of marbled paper to cover the boards. Apply the paper to the boards with spray glue leaving 2 cm (¾ in) extending beyond the short ends and one long edge. Fold the corners, then the allowance to the wrong side.
2. Cut the ribbon in half and stick one end of each of the separate lengths to the middle of the two long covered edges using strong glue. Cut the 'free' ends of the ribbons diagonally.
3. Refer to the diagrams and reinforce the covered corners of the boards with carpet tape. Cut two 32.5 × 25.5 cm (12¾ × 10 in) rectangles of black paper and stick to the wrong side of the boards with spray glue.
4. To make the pockets, cut out two 32.5 × 15 cm (12¾ × 6 in) rectangles of marbled paper for the linings. Apply the linings centrally to the wrong side of two 45 × 20 cm (17¾ × 8 in) rectangles of marbled paper using spray glue. Cut out the pockets following the diagram.
5. Fold the hem on the pockets to the lining and stick in place with double-sided tape. With the linings uppermost, fold the short ends of the pockets towards the lining along the short edges of the lining.
6. Open the pockets out flat again and fold the tabs along the solid lines towards the linings. Now fold the pockets along the broken lines with the right sides facing.
7. Apply double-sided tape to the right side of the tabs. Position the pockets on the black side of the covers over the reinforced corners. Use a weight to hold them in place. Peel off the tape backing to stick the pockets to the covers.
8. Lay one cover right side up on a flat surface. Apply carpet tape along the uncovered edge, overlapping the cover by 1.5 cm (⅝ in) and with 1.5 cm (⅝ in) extending beyond the top and bottom.
9. Stick the other edge of the tape to the uncovered edge of the remaining board, keeping the top and bottom edges level. Turn the tape ends to the inside. Stick tape along the 'hinge' on the inside, sandwiching the edges of the boards. Trim tape ends at the top and bottom edges.

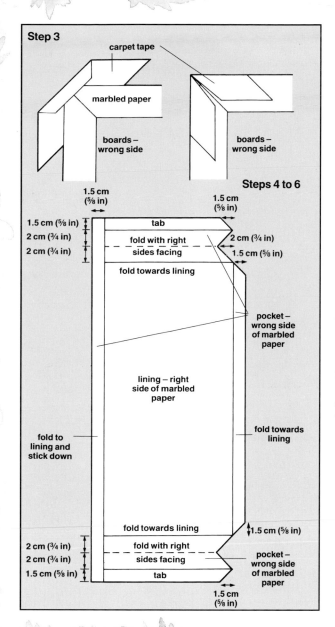

Step 3

carpet tape

marbled paper

boards – wrong side

boards – wrong side

Steps 4 to 6

1.5 cm (⅝ in)

1.5 cm (⅝ in)

1.5 cm (⅝ in)

tab

2 cm (¾ in)

fold with right

2 cm (¾ in)

2 cm (¾ in)

sides facing

1.5 cm (⅝ in)

fold towards lining

pocket – wrong side of marbled paper

lining – right side of marbled paper

fold to lining and stick down

fold towards lining

fold towards lining

1.5 cm (⅝ in)

2 cm (¾ in)

fold with right

2 cm (¾ in)

sides facing

pocket – wrong side of marbled paper

1.5 cm (⅝ in)

tab

1.5 cm (⅝ in)

Initialled book-ends

These 'designer' book-ends will keep any favourite tomes in good order. If you are feeling bold and adventurous, use the initials of a special reader or their beloved author.

Requirements
1.8 cm (¾ in) thick, 9.2 cm (3 ⅝ in) wide softwood
Wood filler
Sandpaper
Four dowels, size 6 mm (¼ in)
Wood glue
2 mm (1/16 in) thick, 8.5 cm (3⅜ in) wide thin plywood
Panel pins
Primer
Spray car paint in white and two contrasting colours
3 mm (⅛ in) thick plywood
Masking tape

Method
1. To make the basic 'L'-shapes of the book-ends, cut two 15 cm (6 in) long pieces of softwood and two 13.5 cm (5¼ in) long pieces. Treat any dents or flaws with wood filler and sandpaper to give a smooth finish.
2. Following the diagram, join the parts together using the dowels and wood glue. Clamp the 'L'-shapes firmly together until set.

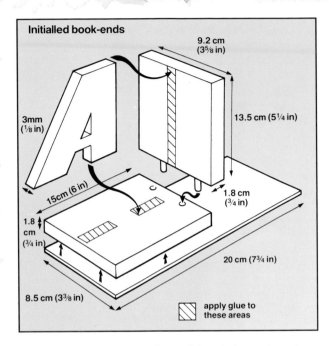

Initialled book-ends

9.2 cm (3⅝ in)

3mm (⅛ in)

13.5 cm (5¼ in)

15cm (6 in)

1.8 cm (¾ in)

1.8 cm (¾ in)

20 cm (7¾ in)

8.5 cm (3⅜ in)

apply glue to these areas

3. Cut two bases from the 2 mm (¹/₁₆ in) plywood, each 20 cm (7¾ in) long. Glue 'L'-shapes to bases following the diagram for positioning. Again, clamp until glue sets – a panel pin at each corner will hold the book-ends still while the clamp is being tightened. Remove all excess glue with a damp cloth. Allow to dry for at least 24 hours.
4. Apply one coat of primer and allow to dry overnight. Sand with a very fine sandpaper.
5. Spray with white car paint in thin coats to avoid runs, allowing each coat to dry before applying the next. To achieve the 'splattered' effect, spray with coloured car paint at close range without shaking the can (contrary to the instructions on the can). It is worth experimenting first on a piece of scrap wood.
6. Using the templates on page 80, cut initials from the 3mm (⅛ in) plywood and spray with contrasting-coloured car paint employing the same method as described above. When dry, fix the initials onto the 'L'-shapes with wood

glue (see the diagram for positioning). Masking tape will hold the initials in place while the glue sets, but remove the tape carefully so that the paint is not lifted. If the paint is damaged, mask the book-ends with newspaper and re-spray. You could decorate your book-ends with alternative 'motifs', using some of the other templates at the end of the book.

Knife block

Keep kitchen knives sharp, handy and safe with this practical yet stylish gift. Choose a finish appropriate to the recipient's home decor: natural wood for a country-style kitchen; a painted, abstract design in primary colours for a modern, 'high-tech' context.

Requirements
1.8 cm (¾ in) thick, 9.2 cm (3⅝ in) wide softwood
4.3 mm (³/₁₆ in) thick, 2.9 cm (1¹/₈ in) wide stripwood
Wood glue
1.2 cm (¹/₂ in) panel pins
Plastic wood
Sandpaper
Clear, eggshell polyurethane varnish
Tracing paper
A soft pencil
Spray car paints
Masking tape

Method
1. Decide how many knives the block is to hold and cut the same number – plus one for the end – of 20 cm (8 in) lengths of softwood.
2. Cut twice as many 20 cm (8 in) lengths of stripwood as the number of knives to be held.
3. Build up the block in sandwich form following the diagram, fixing the stripwood to the softwood with wood glue and panel pins. You can allow space for very broad blades by using narrower stripwood. An attractive colour

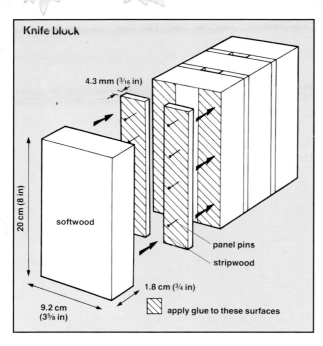

Knife block

4.3 mm (³/₁₆ in)

20 cm (8 in)

softwood

1.8 cm (¾ in)

9.2 cm (3⅝ in)

panel pins

stripwood

▨ apply glue to these surfaces

Blue-jean cafetière cosy

This coffee pot-hugging cosy is made from denim with a quilted lining and closes under the handle with Velcro. Measure your own cafetière first. If it is fatter than our coffee pot, cut a slightly longer piece than the pattern (see page 72-73). It is a good idea to wash the denim to soften it and remove the finish.

Requirements

A 30.5 × 46 cm (12 × 18 in) piece of denim
An 18 × 40.5 cm (7 × 16 in) piece of lining fabric
An 18 × 40.5 cm (7 × 16 in) piece of wadding
A white pencil
Gold-coloured thread
Fray-check liquid or rubber-based glue (contact adhesive)
Velcro

Method

1. Cut out the pattern pieces from denim, lining and wadding (patterns on pages 72-73). A 6 mm (¼ in) seam allowance is included, which should be the width of your sewing machine foot. Put a sharp, strong needle in your machine, since denim is a tough fabric.
2. Draw the two design lines on the pockets with a white pencil and top stitch in gold-coloured thread. Turn under 6 mm (¼ in) from the outer edges of the pocket and top stitch in gold-coloured thread. To prevent the turned-under corners from fraying, apply a fray-check liquid or rubber-based glue. Attach the pockets to the cosy with a line of stitches close to the edges of the pockets. A dab of glue under the corners will help them to stay flat.
3. Top stitch two gold lines down the centre of the cosy 6 mm (¼ in) apart to give the effect of a double seam.
4. Make the belt tags by folding the denim strip in three and machine stitching with gold thread down the centre. Cut the strip into three equal lengths and zig-zag one end of each piece.
5. Place the three belt tags with the unfinished ends just over the line for the waistband. Pin the waistband right

contrast can be achieved by using darker hardwood instead of pale stripwood.
4. When the block is assembled, fill in any dents with plastic wood and sandpaper to give a smooth surface.
5. Apply several coats of clear, eggshell polyurethane varnish for a professional finish.
6. Alternatively, create an interesting and novel finish with paint, in the style of a favourite artist if you like, such as the Mondrian design pictured on pages 42-43. Cut a piece of tracing paper long enough to wrap once around the block. Trace, or sketch freehand, the design using a soft pencil. Position the tracing paper around the block with the reverse of the tracing to the outside and secure with masking tape. Scribble lightly over the reverse of the design's outline to transfer it onto the block. Spray paint the block one colour at a time by masking off areas to be painted in other colours. Follow the manufacturer's instructions on the can.

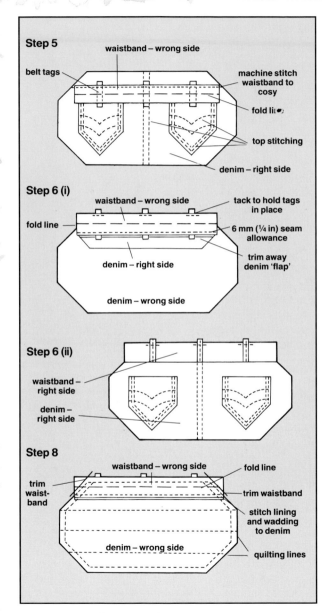

Step 5

waistband – wrong side

belt tags

machine stitch
waistband to
cosy

fold line

top stitching

denim – right side

Step 6 (i)

waistband – wrong side

tack to hold tags
in place

fold line

6 mm (¼ in) seam
allowance

denim – right side

trim away
denim 'flap'

denim – wrong side

Step 6 (ii)

waistband –
right side

denim –
right side

Step 8

trim
waist-
band

waistband – wrong side

fold line

trim waistband

stitch lining
and wadding
to denim

denim – wrong side

quilting lines

side to right side along the marked line and machine.

6. Push up the waistband and tags and press with a steam iron. Tack the ends of the tags to the top of the waistband to hold them in place. The seam allowance should be pressed downwards to make top stitching easier. Trim away the flap of fabric under the waistband.

7. Pin the wadding to the back of the lining and quilt the two together with a few lines of machine stitching.

8. Place lining and denim right side to right side and machine sides and bottom together. Trim off the corners of the waistband and turn the cosy to the right side. Press out corners and edges with your fingers. Do not use an iron at this stage – it will flatten the quilted lining.

9. Fold the waistband over, tucking under a small seam allowance, and machine stitch in gold-coloured thread. This will form the top stitching on the waistband. Hand stitch the ends of the belt tags onto the lining.

10. Sew on a piece of Velcro to close.

Painted silk bow-tie and handkerchief

Making this particular gift allows you the opportunity to create an entirely unique design of your own. Although you may begin with a firm idea, it is hard to be precise in silk painting, so be prepared for a surprising result. We used gold guta to outline the designs. Guta is a blocking agent used to stop the colours running together. There is also a transparent variety of guta which washes out to reveal the original colour of the silk.

Requirements
Tracing paper
A black pen
Masking tape
50 cm (20 in) Habutai or twill silk, washed and ironed
A soft, sharp pencil
Gold guta in a nozzle bottle (same brand as silk paints)

*A frame (an old picture frame, embroidery or adjustable
   frame) with an aperture of at least 30.5 cm (12 in)
   square
A jar of water and a clean cloth
Silk paints in four or five different colours
Paintbrushes, very fine and medium
A piece of scrap cloth
A piece of medium-weight lining fabric
Velcro, if required*

Method

1. The instructions on the tie pattern on page 74 will fit a
37 cm (14½ in) neck size. Increase or decrease the length
of the tie-band as required. If you are uncertain of the neck
size, instead of sewing the two tie pieces together at the
back (see step 12), make the tie-bands long enough to
overlap and fasten with Velcro.
2. Draw out the bow-tie pieces, four in total – two fronts

and two backs – onto tracing paper with a black pen.
When you have decided on your design, draw onto the
tracing. If you feel confident enough, draw freehand
directly onto the silk with the guta (see step 5).
3. Firmly tape the silk over your tracing and using a soft,
sharp pencil, lightly draw the design onto the silk. Check
the straight of grain. Tack the outline of the tie pieces onto
the silk.
4. Use either pins or masking tape to attach the silk to the
frame. Pull until the silk **is** smooth and the design is straight.
5. Draw over the pencil lines with guta onto the silk with
a steady, light hand. The guta tends to start with a blob, so
begin outside the sewing line. Make sure there are no gaps
in the guta for the paint to bleed through. You may find it
easier to apply the guta with a fine paintbrush.
6. Leave to dry – this may take up to 30 minutes. Hold up
to the light and repair any gaps. Again, leave to dry.
7. Have beside you a clean jar of water and a clean cloth.
Read the instructions on the silk paint containers and
shake the paints well. Use a different paintbrush for each
colour. Flood the centre of each area or motif with paint.
Only practice will teach you how much paint to use. Apply
the light colours, then the dark colours. Leave to dry.
8. Cover your ironing board with a spare piece of clean
cloth and iron the painted silk on the wrong side for two
to three minutes to set the paint.
9. Cut out the four tie pieces. Cut out two tie pieces from
the lining fabric.
10. Place the tie pieces on a work surface: one tie back
right side up, one tie front facing down on top of the tie
back, then one tie lining on top of the tie front. Tack, then
machine stitch the pieces together 6 mm (¼ in) from the
edges, leaving the narrow tie-band end open.
11. Turn the tie through to the right side and press under
a clean cloth. Make the other tie portion in the same way.
12. Sew the two tie-bands together, or slip stitch the ends
and sew a piece of Velcro onto the overlap (see step 1).
13. For the handkerchief, cut a piece of silk 35.5 cm (14
in) square. Apply guta and paint in the same way as
described for the bow-tie. Hand roll or machine the edges.

CHAPTER 5

Family Gifts

These are 'activity' gifts, specially designed to involve all members of the family both in their construction and their receipt. The techniques involved in their making are simple enough for the younger members to master and many of the required materials are sure to be found in your store of odd buttons, fabric and paper scraps. Everyone will be entertainingly occupied pitting their creative skills against each other. Our mega cracker provides the perfect answer to inter-family gifts – it can be filled with small gifts and novelties from and for each family member.

52

Christmas stocking family

These fun stockings are made from felt, a user-friendly material since it is easy to handle and does not fray – ideal for children to work with. Each member of the family can make a stocking for another, tailor-made to the individual's personality and their special interests. Turn out your button box, fabric and lace scraps!

Requirements
90 cm (36 in) wide white felt
90 cm (36 in) wide red felt
A pencil
Bonding web
Scraps of fabric for the clown's eyes and mouth
Feather or fur fabric
A pair of pinking shears
Black hat veiling or net
Red narrow ribbon
Black lace
A Christmas cake decoration – holly or bells, etc
Black satin, spotted or tartan ribbon
Rubber-based glue (contact adhesive)
Black and novelty buttons
Narrow coloured ribbon
A novelty eraser and glitter scribble pens

Method

1. Draw the stocking outline (templates on page 75) in pencil on a double layer of felt. Enlarge or reduce the pattern to make different sizes of stocking. Cut out just outside the pencil outline.

2. To make the clown stocking, trace out the clown's eyes and mouth (templates on page 75) in pencil onto the paper side of the bonding web. Cut out just outside the pencil outline. Lay the shapes with the rough (glue) side down on the wrong side of some brightly coloured fabric. Press with a steam iron, leave to cool and then cut on the pencil line to prevent fraying.

3. Peel off backing paper and place features in position on the stocking. Press with the steam iron and leave to cool. Sew on feather or fur fabric eyebrows and hair.

4. Pin the two stocking pieces together, leaving the top open. Using the pencil line as a guide, either machine or hand stitch the two sides together. Trim with pinking shears. You may wish to sew a ribbon loop to the top of the stocking from which to hang it.

5. To make the fishnet and garter stocking, cut two stocking shapes from red felt and one from black hat veiling or net.

6. Pin all three stocking pieces together and machine or hand stitch. Trim with pinking shears.

7. To make the garter, gather a length of black lace and attach to the top front of the stocking. Slip-stitch a length of ribbon down the centre of the lace. Make a bow from the ribbon and attach it, together with a Christmas cake decoration, to one side of the top of the stocking.

8. To make the black tie stocking, follow steps 1 and 4. Make a bow from black satin, spotted or tartan ribbon. A piece of holly or some other decoration may be added to the stocking 'toe'.

9. Make the football stocking from red felt. Glue lengths of ribbon across the stocking in the supporter colours of a favourite team. Glue a football-shaped eraser on the toe.

10. To make the miniature stocking, follow steps 1 and 4. Sew on the novelty buttons and decorate the stocking with glitter scribble pens.

Fancy hats

These inventive hats will set the festive scene for a Christmas dinner party as part of the table decoration, or a celebratory family lunch as part of a mime game to get everyone in a party mood. You can base the designs on the decorative materials in your work box. You can see our designs on pages 52-53 and on the final page of the book.

Requirements

Fairly stiff card in different colours at least 61 cm (24 in) long
A cutting board
A craft knife
A steel ruler
A small stapler
Ribbon, braid, buttons, beads, sequins, offcuts of card and coloured paper, glitter, feathers, etc
Rubber-based glue (contact adhesive)
Double-sided adhesive tape
A black or brown felt-tipped pen

To make the caps

1. Cut a strip of card 61 cm (24 in) long and 3.8 cm (1½ in) wide on a cutting board using a craft knife and a steel ruler. Cut out a cap peak (template on page 77) from the same card. Mark the centre point of the cap peak and band.

2. Heads vary in size of course. You can adjust the fit of the cap band by cutting two slits at either end of the strip – one 2.5 cm (1 in) in length from the top edge and one the same length from the bottom edge – at the appropriate point along the band to form a fastening. You can also use glue.

3. Run a craft knife lightly along the fold line on the wrong side of the peak. This will enable you to fold and curve the peak onto the band. Snip at short intervals into the fold line, taking care not to cut through the fold line.

4. Gently fold the snipped 'seam allowance' towards the wrong side so that the peak will curve.

5. Align the centre marks on the peak and band, hold together between thumb and finger and staple the cap to the band along the snipped 'seam allowance', working from the centre outwards.

6. Decorate the caps with ribbon or strips of paper attached to the cap band to conceal the staples. Add more ribbon, braid, sequins or feathers as you please.

To make Carmen Miranda, maid, peacock and Egyptian hats

1. Cut out the different hat shapes from card (templates on page 77) remembering to cut a band for each 61 cm (24 in) long and 3.8 cm (1½ in) wide as an integral part of the hat shapes.

2. For the maid hat, remember to cut out the triangles and small circles. Using glue, attach black ribbon along the top of the hat band and a bow.

3. For the Carmen Miranda hat, cut out fruit from coloured paper or card (templates on pages 76 and 77). Glue the fruit to the hat in a pleasing arrangement, placing the pineapple in the centre. Glue on the pineapple leaves. Use the felt-tipped pen to add fruit details.

4. For the peacock hat, spray glue a peacock 'eye' feather to the front of the hat. Add pieces of decorative paper either side of the feather – perhaps two peacock 'eye' feathers cut from a paper napkin, as we did.

5. For the Egyptian hat, cut a piece of gold corrugated card to cover the front of the hat. Attach with glue. Cut a 4 cm (1½ in) diameter circle from red card and glue to the centre of the hat band. Add coloured beads to look like jewels along the hat band.

HINTS

Card marks easily, especially gold card, so it is a good idea to remove any jewellery before you begin. You could devise a game in which your guests have to act in the manner of their hat. The hats could then be switched so that everyone has a turn in the different hats.

Christmas board game

The whole family will be entertained over the festive period re-living the horrors and happiness of December past as they progress up the tree, in fits and starts, towards Christmas Day. The first to reach number 25 will be the winner. They are sure to enjoy devising their own 'pleasures' and 'pitfalls', each carrying a reward or forfeit respectively.

Requirements

A 59.4 × 42 cm (A2 or 22½ × 16½ in) piece of card; or two 42 × 29.7 cm (A3 or 16½ × 11¼ in) pieces 'hinged' by pieces of adhesive tape at the back
A 59.4 × 42 cm (A2 or 22½ × 16½ in) piece of scrap paper
A 59.4 × 42 cm (A2 or 22½ × 16½ in) piece of green paper
Spray glue
A silver pen
Self-adhesive spots in three colours
A black felt-tipped pen
A small piece of silver paper
Coloured counters, one for each player
Dice and a shaker

Method

1. Fold the scrap paper in half lengthways and draw one half of a Christmas tree outline up to the fold. Cut round the outline through both thicknesses of paper to make a symmetrical tree shape.

2. Draw round the perimeter of the tree template onto green paper and cut out. Glue onto the card (you will need to cut the tree into two pieces if you are using two 'hinged' pieces of card for the base board).

3. Draw 'tinsel' garlands strung from branch to branch across the tree with silver pen.

4. Choosing a different colour for the odd and even numbers, number the self-adhesive spots 1 to 24 using a black felt-tipped pen. Position the spots at intervals along

the garlands, placing an unmarked spot in a third colour between each numbered spot. Position the last spot – numbered 24 – 14 cm (5½ in) below the apex of the tree.

5. Cut out a star from silver paper (template on page 73) or white paper coloured with the silver pen. Write the number 25 in black pen in the centre of the star, or colour a white spot with the silver pen and position on the star. Glue the star to the top of the tree. Now play the game. Each player (any number) must throw a six to begin.

Pleasures – odd numbers

1 You can begin to eat your chocolate advent calendar.
3 You receive your first Christmas card.
5 St Nicholas' Day (December 5).

7 You are chosen to be the front half of the horse in the pantomime!
9 Your carol singing raises a record sum of money for charity.
11 You successfully complete your hand crafted gifts.
13 A long lost friend telephones to invite you to her Christmas feast.
15 A visit to Santa in his grotto at the local store.
17 End of the school term.
19 Time to decorate the Christmas tree.
21 You receive a surprise mystery parcel from overseas.
23 You discover that your long lost friend is of cordon bleu status!
Rewards: go to St Nicholas' Day; go forward three spots; have two throws; nominate another player to join you; join the player nearest to December 25

Pitfalls – even numbers

2 You burn the Christmas cake.
4 You are chosen to be the rear half of the horse in the pantomime!
6 People do not appreciate your carol singing and bombard you with rotten fruit rather than cash.
8 The Christmas tree will not fit through the front door.
10 You receive an unexpected bill.
12 The dog eats the tree decorations.
14 You are given a difficult school project to do over the vacation.
16 You receive a singing card from your wealthy aunt overseas instead of a 'proper' gift.
18 The dog eats your gifts for the family.
20 You find your Christmas gift list which you clearly forgot to send to Santa.
22 Long lost relatives come to stay.
24 You discover that your oven is too small for your Christmas dinner!
Forfeits: wait a turn; wait to throw a six; go back three spots; go to December 1; join the player nearest the beginning of December; nominate another player to join you

Mega cracker

A giant Christmas cracker will make an eye-catching centrepiece for the festive table, colour-coordinated with napkins and table-mats. This cracker is re-usable, so with care it will last indefinitely. The family will have great fun re-decorating it year after year, adding new snaps, collecting miniature gifts to put inside and writing mottoes from their store of jokes.

You will need to search the supermarket for two suitable tubular packages, one slightly larger than the other. These will be used as 'former' tubes to shape the cracker, so they must be firm.

Requirements

Thin white card
Two former tubes about 10 cm (4 in) in diameter – one
 must be slightly smaller in diameter than the other
A stapler – check that it is full
Two snaps joined together with adhesive tape
Rubber-based glue (contact adhesive)
Two 34 × 51 cm (13½ × 20 in) pieces of crepe paper
Fine string
Green giftwrap ribbon
Red 'lace' border ribbon with gathering thread
A 20 × 70 cm (8 × 27½ in) piece of gold paper
A ruler
A craft knife
Satin ribbon for the lily
Fray-check liquid
A few shiny round beads
Fine wire
Self-adhesive paper spots
Gifts and mottoes

Method

1. Cut four pieces of card, two 13 × 34 cm (5 × 13½ in), one 20 × 34 cm (8 × 13½ in) and one 19 × 32 cm (7½ × 12½ in). The card will bend more smoothly in one direction, so experiment first with a spare piece of card.

2. Roll the 19 × 32 cm (7½ × 12½ in) card around the smaller of the two formers, mark lightly with a pencil where the long edges meet and overlap, slide the former back so that the card overhangs the former and, holding firmly with the stapler upside-down, punch a staple into the card to hold the overlapping edges together. The smooth side of the staple will then be inside the tube. Slide out the former, continue to hold firmly and staple the overlapping card along its length. If the stapler will not

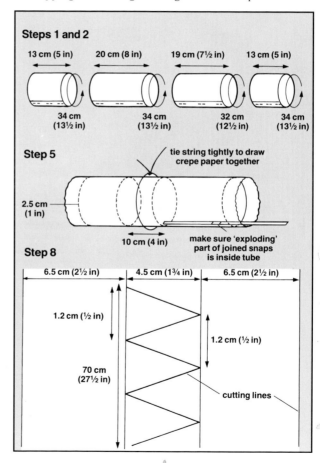

Steps 1 and 2
13 cm (5 in) 20 cm (8 in) 19 cm (7½ in) 13 cm (5 in)
34 cm (13½ in) 34 cm (13½ in) 32 cm (12½ in) 34 cm (13½ in)

Step 5
tie string tightly to draw crepe paper together
2.5 cm (1 in)
10 cm (4 in)
make sure 'exploding' part of joined snaps is inside tube

Step 8
6.5 cm (2½ in) 4.5 cm (1¾ in) 6.5 cm (2½ in)
1.2 cm (½ in)
1.2 cm (½ in)
70 cm (27½ in)
cutting lines

reach the centre, use adhesive tape. Make the other three tubes in the same way but using the slightly larger former.

3. Place the joined snaps inside the longer of the two centre tubes. Fold one end over the rim of the tube and hold in place with a dab of glue. Make sure that the snap itself is inside the tube – see diagram for step 5.

4. Lay out one sheet of crepe paper. Lightly glue along one long edge. Place one short tube and the longer of the two centre tubes on the paper, leaving 2.5 cm (1 in) to tuck into the short tube and 10 cm (4 in) between the tubes. Slide the largest former inside the tubes.

5. Firmly roll the crepe paper around the tubes, making sure the join is over the staples. Check that the glue has not stuck to the former. Glue the excess crepe paper overhanging the short tube and tuck into the tube. When the glue is dry, gently slide the former level with the rim of the long tube and tie a piece of string tightly between the two tubes to draw up the crepe paper. Trim the string. Gently remove the former and tuck in the remaining excess crepe paper overhanging the long tube. Pinch firmly to make a crisp fold, then gently unfold the paper from the tube, apply glue and tuck back inside the tube.

6. Repeat steps 4 and 5 to make the other end of the cracker, using the smaller former so that the second centre tube will fit inside the first centre tube.

7. Glue the giftwrap ribbon to the outer edges of the cracker. Pull the thread to gather the 'lace' ribbon and tie the resulting frills around the 'waists' of the cracker.

8. To make the pointed borders from the gold paper, measure three lines 6.5 cm (2½ in), 11 cm (4¼ in) and 17.5 cm (6¾ in) from the long edge. Measure and mark the first two lines at 1.2 cm (½ in) intervals. Join up the marks to make a zig-zag line – see the diagram. Cut along the zig-zag and outside lines using a craft knife and steel ruler to create the two borders. Glue the straight edges to butt against the ribbon around the ends of the cracker. When the glue is dry, gently lift points and glue in place.

9. Draw out six lily petals (template on page 80) on the back of the satin ribbon. Lightly smear with fray-check liquid. Leave to dry and cut out petals.

10. Thread the beads onto fine wire, twist then wrap the lily petals around them and secure with wire.

11. Cut out leaves from giftwrap ribbon, wrap around lily and secure with a dot of glue. Attach the lily to the centre of the cracker with glue.

12. Place spots above the points of the gold paper borders.

13. When you have filled the cracker, slide the narrower centre tube into the wider tube with the snap sandwiched between the two interlocking tubes. Stick the 'free' end of the snap to the outside of the cracker with glue.

CHAPTER 6

Gift Cards & Boxes

It is always fun and rewarding to create your own cards rather than purchasing the mass-produced variety. Hand-crafted, they become gifts in themselves for absent friends and relatives to treasure. One of our card ideas actually incorporates a separate gift – a pair of hand-made earrings – as part of the overall design. Customized packaging adds another dimension to any gift. You can increase the mystery value by disguising the shape of the item in a giftbox. You can also transform any rectangular package into a seasonal 'character' to entertain the children, like our red-nosed reindeer giftbox.

Rocking cards

Have fun making this pair of jolly, rocking cards for Christmas. Hand-made greeting cards are always extra special and this duo can be brought out each year as amusing decorations.

Requirements
A compass
Pink card
Blue card
Two 21.5 cm (8½ in) diameter white doilies
Spray glue
A craft knife
Beige card
A brown felt-tipped pen
Household glue
White sugar
Dark brown card
White card
Red card
Green card

Method
1. Cut out a 24 cm (9½ in) diameter circle from pink and blue card. Apply the doilies centrally on the circles with spray glue. Score across the middle of the back of the circles with a craft knife and fold in half.
2. To make the sweet mincemeat pies, cut out three bases and three tops from beige card (templates on page 71). Draw a cross in the centre of the tops with the brown felt-tipped pen. Glue the tops to the bases.
3. Spread glue on top of the pies and sprinkle with sugar. Shake off the excess, then glue the pies to the front of the pink semi-circle, positioning the pies symmetrically so that the card is not weighted down on one side.
4. Cut out a 13.5 cm (5⅜ in) diameter circle of dark brown card for the Christmas pudding. Cut out the 'cream' in white card (template on page 71) and glue to the pudding. Glue the pudding centrally to the front of the blue semi-circle.
5. Cut out three berries in red card and two holly leaves in green card (templates on page 71). Score across the centre of the leaves and bend in half. Glue the berries and leaves to the top of the pudding.

Earring cards

A jewellery gift forms an integral part of the design of these cards – an ideal gift for an absent friend. The earring bases are similar to covered buttons. They can be purchased (see page 68 for supplier) in a variety of sizes, for both pierced and non-pierced ears, ready-covered in felt – either red for the holly berries or white for the mistletoe berries.

If you want to create your own design with different

> **HINT**
> *Button earrings need not masquerade as berries – they can be wheels, baubles, balloons or bubbles. You will have fun creating variations on this card.*

coloured earrings as part of the overall scheme, the white felt earring bases can be dyed a wide range of different colours using fabric dyes. Carefully follow the manufacturer's instructions supplied with the dyes.

Requirements
Ready-covered button-style earring bases (see page 68 for supplier) – mail-order service available
A beading needle
White and red sewing thread
A selection of tiny beads, star sequins, cup sequins, rocaille and bugal beads in white and red
Ready-made card 'blanks' or a piece of silver and a piece of blue card
Green paper for leaves
A dark brown or black felt-tipped pen for drawing the mistletoe stem

Method
1. Using a beading needle and white thread, cover the white felt earring bases with white beads, sequins, and French knots until they are completely filled. Hold the sequins in place by sewing a bead slightly larger in size than the sequin hole in the centre of the sequin and threading back through the sequin hole.
2. Cover the red felt earring bases with red beads, sequins and French knots in the same way.
3. Cut silver card 30.5 × 20 cm (12 × 8 in) for the holly card and fold in half widthways. Cut three holly leaves from green paper (template on page 75). Gently fold each leaf in half. Apply glue to the fold on the back of the leaves and attach them to the card. Cut a slit or cross where the 'berries' are to be positioned, insert the backs of the earrings through the holes and fasten.
4. Cut blue card 23 × 18 cm (9 × 7 in) for the mistletoe card and fold in half widthways. Cut four leaves from green paper, two from each template (see page 75) and gently fold each leaf in half. Draw a stem on the card before attaching the leaves with glue. Mount the earrings as described above.

A red-nosed reindeer giftbox

This comical reindeer will delight the children and there is an added surprise because the reindeer also disguises a Christmas present.

Requirements
Chestnut brown giftwrap paper
Four small boxes
Household glue
Spray glue
Beige card
A craft knife
A red bead
Scraps of white, black and blue card

Method
1. Wrap a gift in a rectangular box with the giftwrap paper. Also wrap four small boxes for the legs and glue these under the large box.
2. Stick two 20 cm (8 in) squares of giftwrap paper together with spray glue and cut out a pair of ears and one tail (templates on page 69). Bend the tabs towards the ears and then glue to the top of the box 5 cm (2 in) from the front, with the top tab glued on top of the box and the side tab glued to the side of the box.
3. Fold the tail into thirds along the fold lines and glue together at the top. Cut a fringe through all three thicknesses. Glue the tail to the back of the box.
4. Cut out a pair of antlers from beige card (template on page 69) and score lightly along the broken lines with a craft knife. Bend the tabs backwards along the scored lines. Glue the tabs to the top of the box behind the ears.
5. To make the muzzle, cut one muzzle in card and one in giftwrap paper (template on page 69), cutting the paper along the broken lines. Apply the card muzzle to the back of the paper muzzle with spray glue.
6. Bend the muzzle into a cone shape with the straight card edges meeting edge to edge. Glue the paper overlap in place to secure the cone.

7. Snip the paper circumference to the card at 1 cm (3/8 in) intervals and then glue the snipped edges inside the cone. Bend the tabs backwards at right angles to the cone and glue to the front of the box. Dab the point of the nose with glue and push it into the hole in the bead. Hold the bead in place while the glue sets.
8. Cut out two eyes from white card, two irises and two sets of eyelashes from black card and two eyelids from blue card (templates on page 69). Glue the irises and lids to the eyes. Cut a fringe on the eyelashes and glue the top edge to the lids. Gently bend the lashes upwards. Glue the eyes to each side of the box.

Christmas tree giftbox

Here is an elegant giftbox for a special present. Place the gift in the gold 'tub' and finish off with a green cone lid trimmed with a garland of gold beads. The giftbox is simple enough for you to make one for each of your yuletide guests and would look charming on the Christmas dinner table at each place setting or grouped together on the mantlepiece or sideboard.

Requirements
Green card
Gold card
A craft knife
Double-sided adhesive tape
Gold beads
Sewing thread
Transparent adhesive tape

Method
1. Use the templates on page 70 to cut out a tree from green card and a tub from gold card. Score each piece on the back along the dashed lines with a craft knife and bend the sections forward along the scored lines.
2. Stick the tab on the tree under the opposite end with double-sided adhesive tape to form a cone. Now stick the end tab on the tub under the opposite end and the base tabs inside the tub with double-sided adhesive tape.
3. Thread a needle with a long length of thread. Knot the thread ends together and push the needle up through the apex of the tree. Place the tree on the tub and thread on the beads. Drape the beads around the tree and stick the ends of the thread to the underside of the cone with transparent adhesive tape.

> **HINT**
> *Alternatively, make the cone from brightly-coloured glossy card and drape a length of fine gold tinsel (trimmed if too thick) around the tree.*

Miniature boxes

These tiny boxes are specially designed to carry precious gifts. Made of silk or lawn and sewn by hand, they could hold a piece of jewellery, theatre tickets, bath oil capsules or cash. They can be closed with narrow ribbon or trimmed with a tassel.

Requirements

A piece of iron-on buckram (Vilene) approximately 30 cm (12 in) square
Small quantities of silk or lawn
Tacking and matching thread – silk thread is very good for hand sewing
Narrow ribbon
Embroidery silk for the tassel
A 5 cm (2 in) square piece of card

Method

1. To make the hexagonal boxes, use the templates on page 78 and cut the following pieces from the buckram (Vilene): four hexagon shapes – one fractionally smaller than the size given (for the base lining), two slightly larger (for the lid and its lining) and one the exact size given (for the outer base); six rectangles for the outer sides and six rectangles slightly smaller than the size given, for lining the sides. Label the pieces on the 'unglued' side so that they do not become muddled.

2. Position the buckram (Vilene) pieces, 'glue'-side down, on the wrong side of the piece of silk or lawn, making sure there is a 6 mm (¼ in) seam allowance around each piece. Press all the pieces with a steam iron, leave to cool and cut out with the seam allowances.

3. Starting with a double stitch rather than a knot (to facilitate removal), fold over the seam allowance of the fabric and tack to the buckram (Vilene). Complete all pieces in the same way. If you are planning to use silk thread for the final stitching, tack also in silk so that no holes are left in the fabric after you have removed the tacking stitches.

4. Press all the pieces. Take the outer hexagon base and one outer side. Place them right side to right side and sew one side of the rectangle to one side of the hexagon with small stitches. Continue in the same way with the other five outer sides.

5. Push the sides upright and join together with a ladder or slip stitch sewn from the right side. You have now completed the outer box.

6. Follow steps 4 and 5 to make the lining box, except in this case the right side should be inside the box. Therefore, sew from the wrong side.

7. Gently insert the lining box into the outer box and ladder or slip stitch the two together along the top edge. Take out the tacking stitches.

8. Tack the outer lid and lining, then slip stitch them together around all six sides. Take out the tacking and stitch one side of the lid to the top edge of one side of the hexagon box.

9. Sew on two lengths of narrow ribbon, one to the box and one to the lid, to tie and close the box.

10. To make the diamond box, follow the instructions above but working with four sides rather than six.

11. To make the tassel, wrap embroidery silk round the card several times. Tie a piece of embroidery silk around the loops at one end. Gently slide the skein off the card and just below the tied end, wind a length of silk round the skein, knot and pull through to hold. Trim the ends of the silk. Trim off the loops at the other end of the skein in a straight line. Trim the ends of the tied embroidery silk at the top of the tassel and hand sew to the front 'point' of the diamond lid.

> **HINT**
> *We have given two alternative patterns for the hexagonal box (see page 78) – one for a shallow box, the other for a deeper-sided version. But you can enlarge or reduce the patterns on a photocopier, or by using the grid, to tailor-make boxes to fit your special gifts.*

List of suppliers

United Kingdom

All Plants and Sundries Ltd
167 Handcroft Road
Croydon, Surrey

Boudicca Dried Flowers
Unit 12, First Avenue
Bluebridge Industrial Estate
Halstead, Surrey

Canonbury Art Shop and Picture Framers
271 Upper Street, London N1

Cooks Graphic Art Warehouse
117 Long Acre, London WC2

*Craft Creations Ltd
Unit 7, Harpers Yard
Ruskin Road, Tottenham
London N17

Cromartie Hobbycraft Ltd
Park Hall Road, Longton
Stoke-on-Trent
Staffordshire ST3 5AY

*Culpepper Ltd
Herbs
34 Bruton Place
London W1

Daler Board Co Ltd
Paper, card, picture frames
East Street, Wareham
Dorset BH20 4NT

Ells and Farrier Ltd
Beads and sequins
20 Princes Street
Hanover Square
London W1

Falkiner Fine Papers Ltd
76 Southampton Row
London WC1

General Woodwork Supplies
76 Stoke Newington High Street
London N16

*Handicraft Shop
Northgate, Canterbury, Kent CT1 1BE

Harlequin
Covered earring bases, page 63
Jubilee End, Lawford
Manningtree
Essex CO11 1UR

John Lewis Partnership
Fabric, ribbons, haberdashery
278–306 Oxford Street
London W1

*Magpie Patchworks
Dept G, 37 Palfrey Road
Northbourne
Bournemouth
Dorset BN10 6DN

Maple Textiles
188–190 Maple Road
London SE20

Offray Ribbons Ltd
Ribbon for slippers, page 45
Fir Tree Place, Church Road
Ashford, Middlesex

The Quilt Room
20 West Street, Dorking
Surrey RH4 1BL

*Paperchase Products Ltd
213 Tottenham Court Road
London W1

Pioneer Patches
Patchwork fabrics
Marsh Mills, Luck Lane
Huddersfield HD3 4AB

Reeves Art Shop
178 Kensington High Street
London W8

The Reject Shop
Picture frames
245 Brompton Road
London SW3

George Rowney and Co Ltd
Artists' materials
12 Percy Street
London W1

*Silken Strands
Threads and beads
33 Linksway, Gatley
Cheadle, Cheshire SK8 4LA

Snaphappy
Cracker materials, gifts and mottoes, page 58
Unit 5, Viables Craft Centre
Harrow Way, Basingstoke
Hants RG22 4BJ

Swan Craft Gallery
Floral materials and creations
Roman Road
Ashfield Cum Thorpe
Suffolk IP14 6LU

George Weil & Sons
Silk and silk paints
The Warehouse
Reading Arch Road
Redhill RH1 1HG

*mail order service available

Australia

ACI Timber and Building Supplies
19 Seven Hills Road
Seven Hills, Sydney
New South Wales

All Handcraft Supplies
101 Warringah Mall
Brookvale, Sydney
New South Wales

Artdraft
120 Rowe Street
Eastwood, Sydney
New South Wales

Calico and Lace
368 Pacific Highway
Lindfield, Sydney
New South Wales

Dried Flowers International
31 Warraba Road
North Narrabeen
Sydney
New South Wales

Flowerama
Unit G1, Industrial Estate
Cnr Windsor Road and Victoria Avenue
Castle Hill, Sydney
New South Wales

Flower World
465 Spencer Street
West Melbourne
Victoria

Fremantle Crafts and Supplies
255 South Terrace
South Fremantle, Perth
West Australia

Hobbytex
5 Victoria Avenue
Castle Hill, Sydney
New South Wales

Kelmscott Hobbies Arts and Crafts
17 Denny Avenue, Kelmscott
Perth, West Australia

Melbourne Handicraft Supplies
103 Puckle, Moonee Ponds
Melbourne
Victoria

Rosemary Herb Farm
Strachan Road, Bullsbrook
Perth
West Australia

Simply Stitches
Rear 387 Victoria Avenue
Chatswood, Sydney
New South Wales

Tait Timber and Hardware Pty
45 Grant Road
Somerville, Melbourne
Victoria

Things Wild
75 Rokeby Road, Subiaco
Perth, West Australia

The Work Basket
27 Bruce, Nadlands
Perth
West Australia

Templates and patterns

The patterns and templates in white are actual size. Those coloured blue are reduced in size. To enlarge, draw a grid of 1.4 cm (9⁄16 in) squares, then copy the shapes onto your grid, square by square, using the grid lines as a guide. Alternatively, enlarge the patterns on a photocopier to 141% (or A4 enlarged to A3). Only half the pattern of symmetrical shapes may be printed. To make a complete pattern, place the actual size pattern onto a piece of folded paper, with the dashed line to the fold, and cut out.

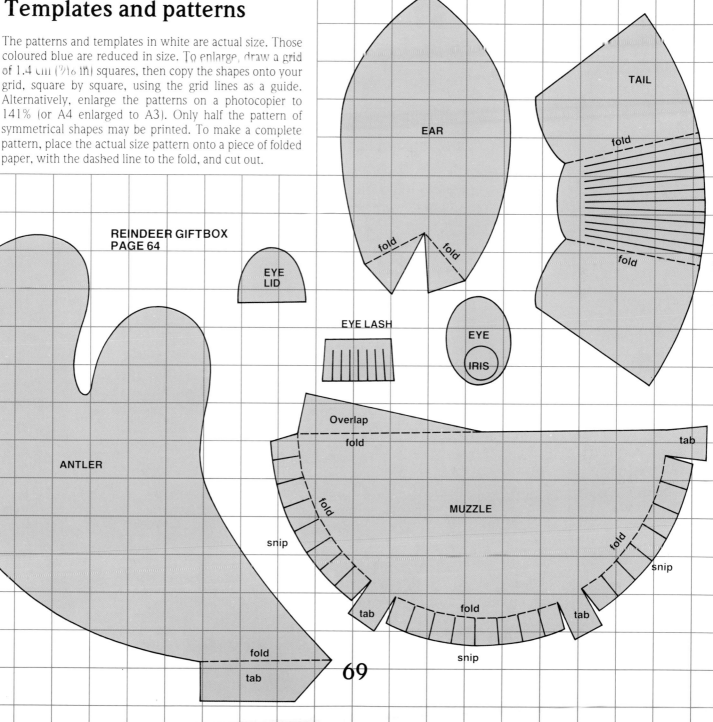

REINDEER GIFTBOX
PAGE 64

EAR

TAIL

EYE LID

EYE LASH

EYE

IRIS

ANTLER

fold

tab

Overlap

fold

fold

MUZZLE

snip

fold

tab

snip

tab

fold

fold

snip

tab

snip

69

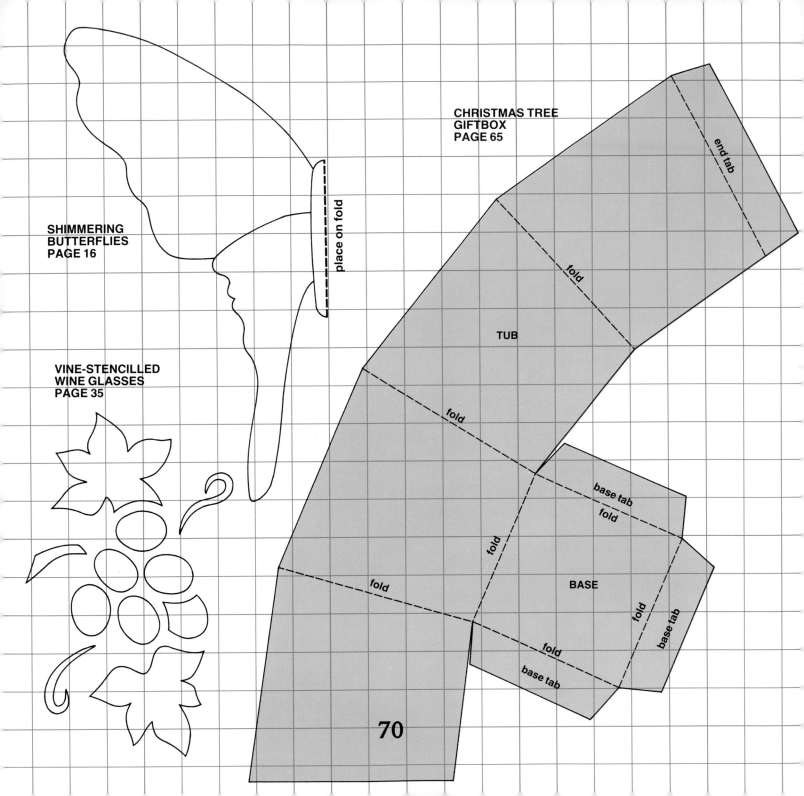

SHIMMERING
BUTTERFLIES
PAGE 16

VINE-STENCILLED
WINE GLASSES
PAGE 35

place on fold

CHRISTMAS TREE
GIFTBOX
PAGE 65

end tab

fold

TUB

fold

base tab

fold

fold

BASE

fold

base tab

fold

base tab

70

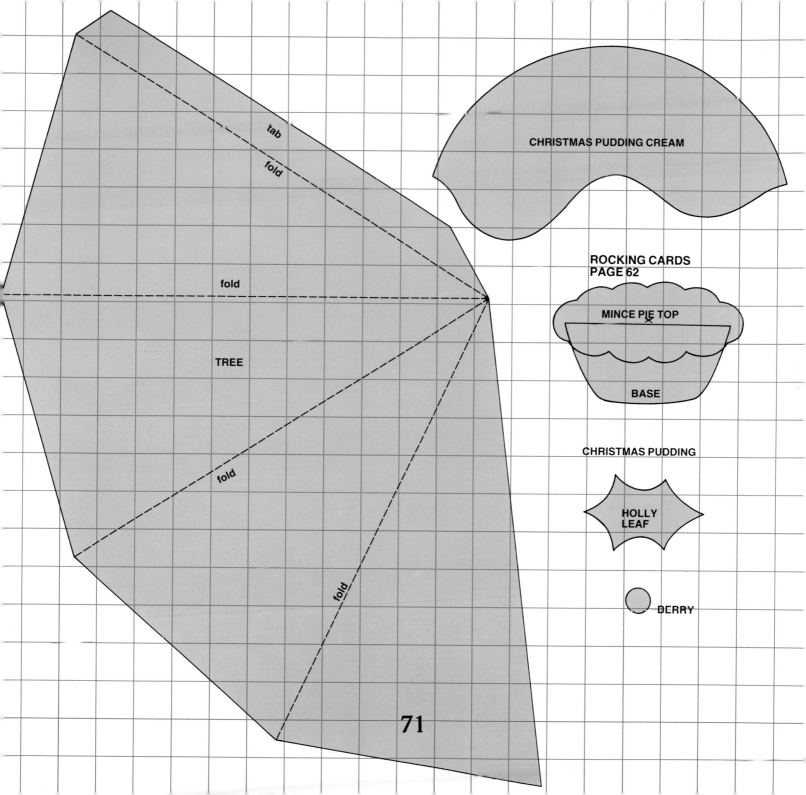

tab

fold

fold

TREE

fold

fold

71

CHRISTMAS PUDDING CREAM

ROCKING CARDS
PAGE 62

MINCE PIE TOP

BASE

CHRISTMAS PUDDING

HOLLY
LEAF

BERRY

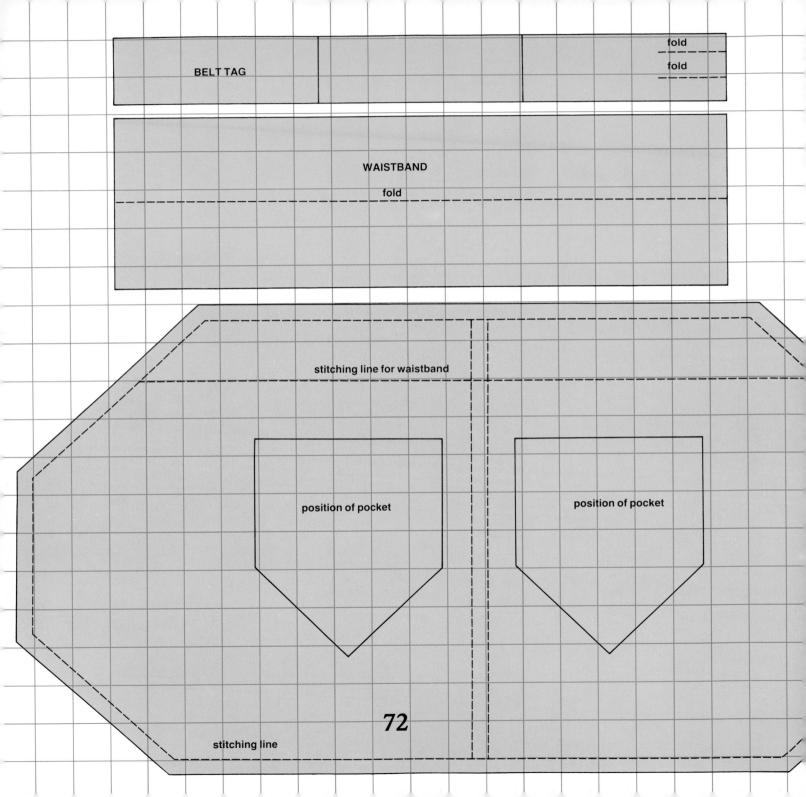

BELT TAG

WAISTBAND

fold

stitching line for waistband

position of pocket

position of pocket

72

stitching line

fold

fold

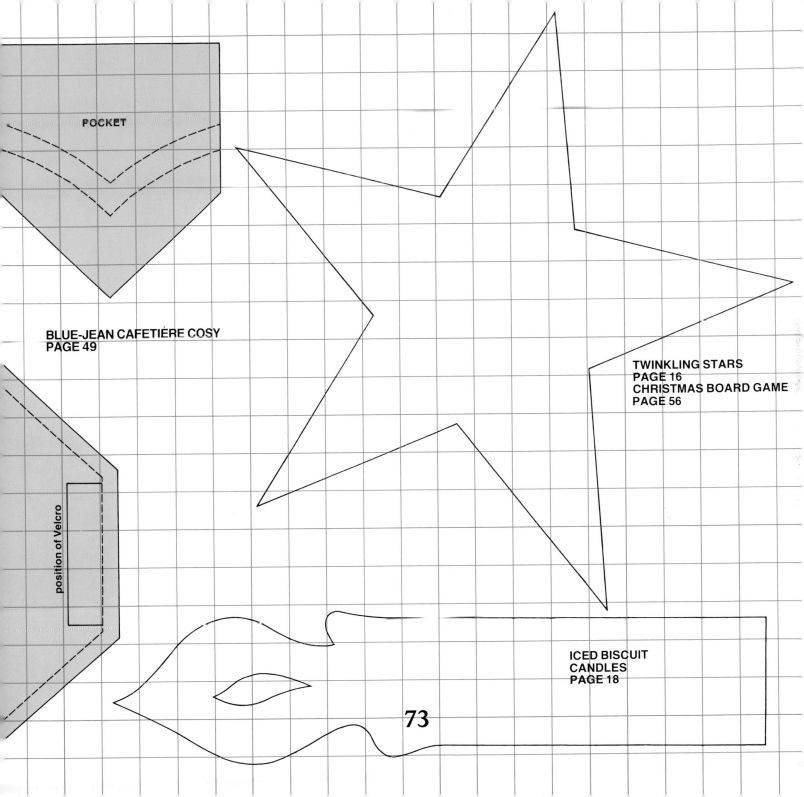

POCKET

BLUE-JEAN CAFETIÈRE COSY
PAGE 49

position of Velcro

TWINKLING STARS
PAGE 16
CHRISTMAS BOARD GAME
PAGE 56

ICED BISCUIT
CANDLES
PAGE 18

73

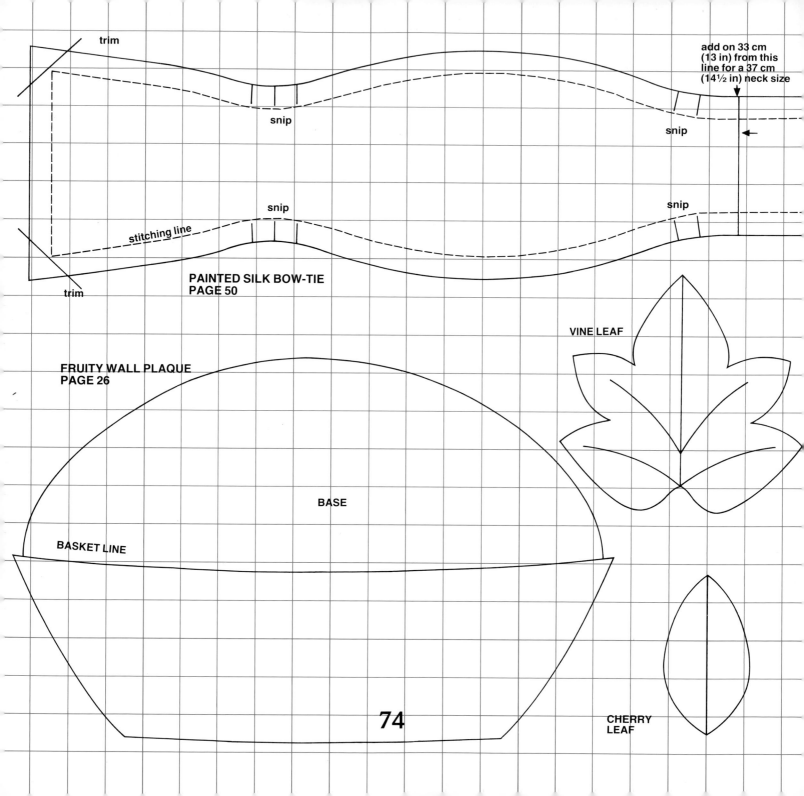

trim

add on 33 cm
(13 in) from this
line for a 37 cm
(14½ in) neck size

snip

snip

snip

snip

stitching line

trim

**PAINTED SILK BOW-TIE
PAGE 50**

VINE LEAF

**FRUITY WALL PLAQUE
PAGE 26**

BASE

BASKET LINE

74

**CHERRY
LEAF**

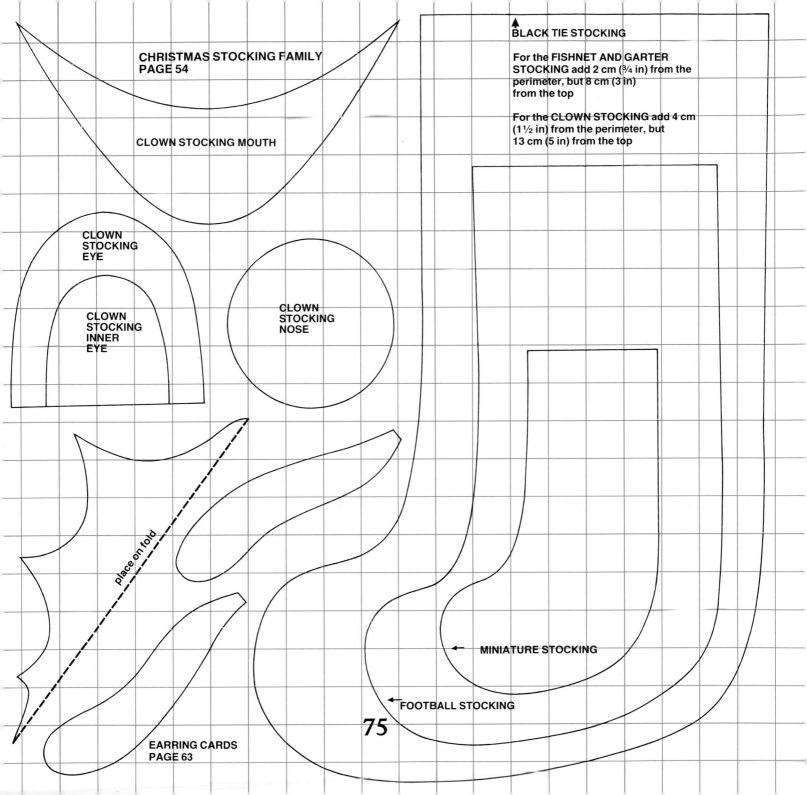

CHRISTMAS STOCKING FAMILY
PAGE 54

CLOWN STOCKING MOUTH

BLACK TIE STOCKING

For the FISHNET AND GARTER
STOCKING add 2 cm (¾ in) from the
perimeter, but 8 cm (3 in)
from the top

For the CLOWN STOCKING add 4 cm
(1½ in) from the perimeter, but
13 cm (5 in) from the top

CLOWN
STOCKING
EYE

CLOWN
STOCKING
INNER
EYE

CLOWN
STOCKING
NOSE

place on fold

MINIATURE STOCKING

FOOTBALL STOCKING

75

EARRING CARDS
PAGE 63

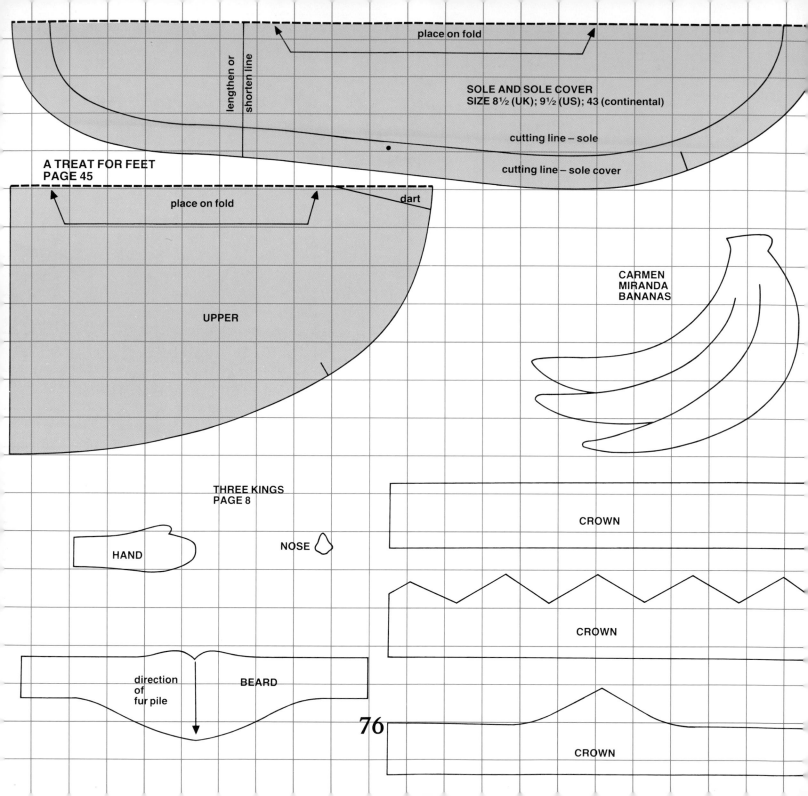

place on fold

lengthen or shorten line

SOLE AND SOLE COVER
SIZE 8½ (UK); 9½ (US); 43 (continental)

cutting line – sole

cutting line – sole cover

A TREAT FOR FEET
PAGE 45

place on fold

dart

UPPER

CARMEN MIRANDA BANANAS

THREE KINGS
PAGE 8

CROWN

HAND

NOSE

CROWN

direction of fur pile

BEARD

76

CROWN

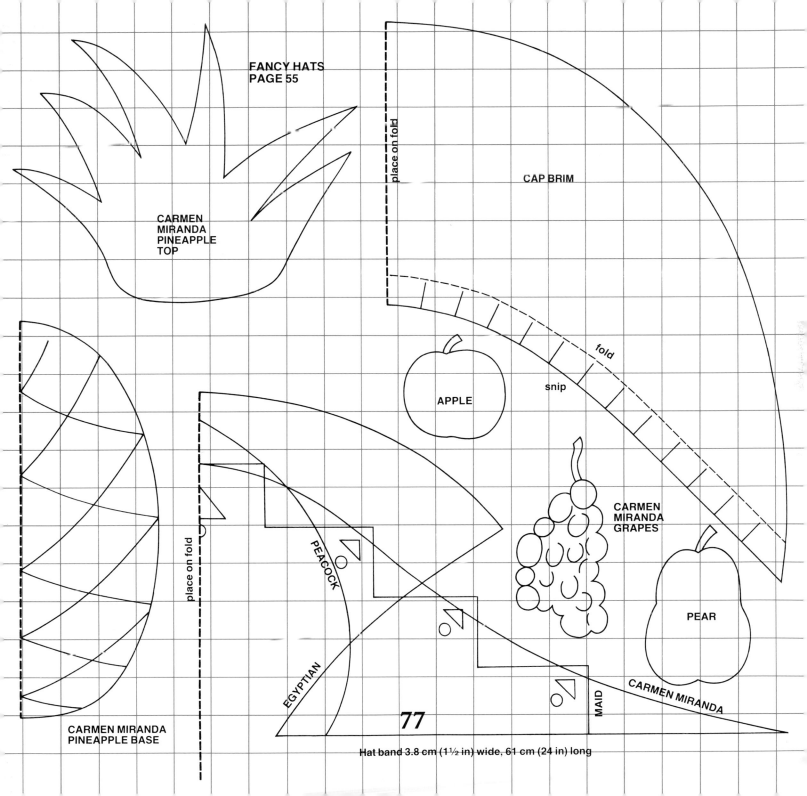

**FANCY HATS
PAGE 55**

CARMEN
MIRANDA
PINEAPPLE
TOP

place on fold

CAP BRIM

fold

snip

APPLE

CARMEN
MIRANDA
GRAPES

PEACOCK

place on fold

EGYPTIAN

PEAR

CARMEN MIRANDA

MAID

77

CARMEN MIRANDA
PINEAPPLE BASE

Hat band 3.8 cm (1½ in) wide, 61 cm (24 in) long

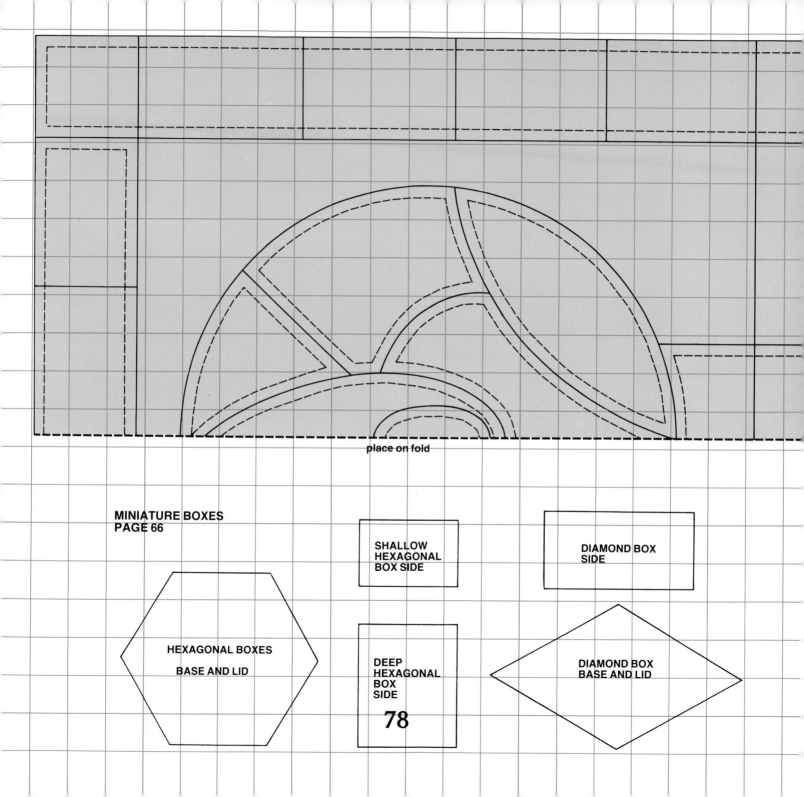

place on fold

MINIATURE BOXES
PAGE 66

SHALLOW
HEXAGONAL
BOX SIDE

DIAMOND BOX
SIDE

HEXAGONAL BOXES

BASE AND LID

DEEP
HEXAGONAL
BOX
SIDE

78

DIAMOND BOX
BASE AND LID

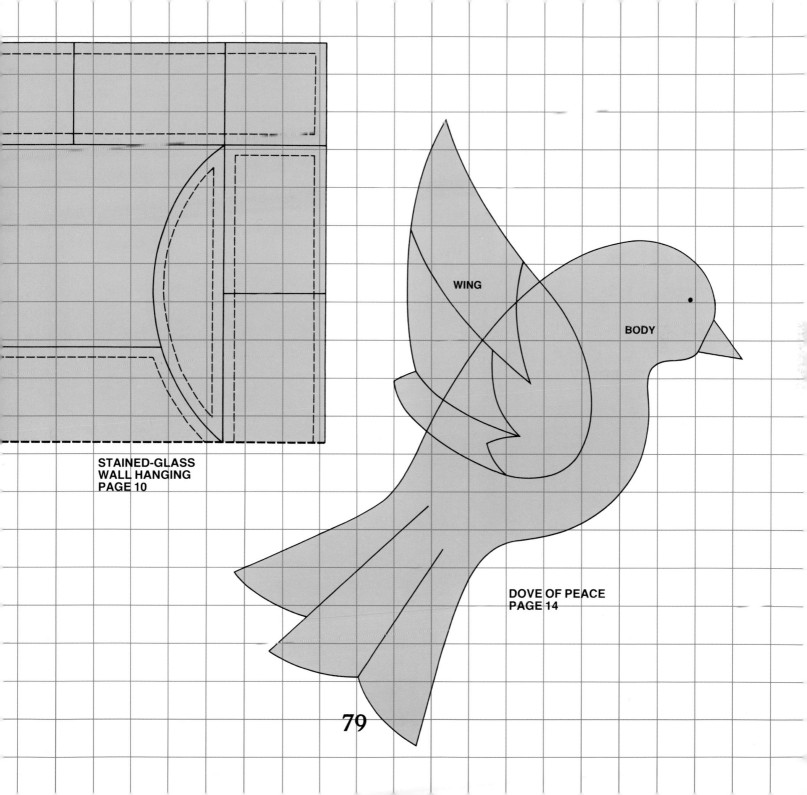

STAINED-GLASS
WALL HANGING
PAGE 10

WING

BODY

DOVE OF PEACE
PAGE 14

79

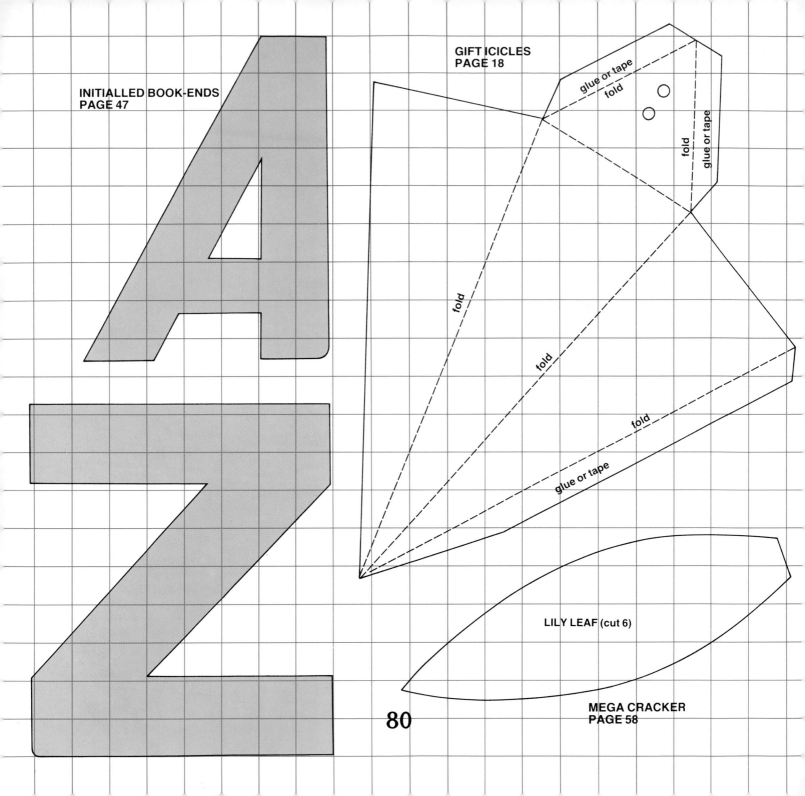

INITIALLED BOOK-ENDS
PAGE 47

GIFT ICICLES
PAGE 18

glue or tape

fold

fold

glue or tape

fold

fold

fold

glue or tape

LILY LEAF (cut 6)

80

MEGA CRACKER
PAGE 58

Fancy hats, page 55